A Pattern
for Failure

A Pattern for Failure

Socialist Economies in Crisis

Sven Rydenfelt

Introduction by Milton Friedman

 HARCOURT BRACE JOVANOVICH, PUBLISHERS

San Diego   New York   London

LIBRARY OF CONGRESS CATALOGING IN PUBLICATION DATA

Rydenfelt, Sven.
A pattern for failure.
Translation of: Bönder, mat, socialism.
Bibliography: p.
Includes index.
1. Communist countries—Economic conditions—Case
studies.   2. Agriculture and state—Communist countries—
Case studies.   3. Socialism—Case studies.   4. Central
planning—Case studies.   I. Title.
HC704.R9313 1985   330.9171'7   84-12909
ISBN 0-15-171333-2

Printed in the United States of America

Designed by Karen Savary

First edition

A   B   C   D   E

Unless we can make the philosophical foundations of a free society once more a living intellectual issue, and its implementation a task which challenges the ingenuity and imagination of our liveliest minds, the prospects of freedom are indeed dark. But if we can regain the belief in the power of ideas which was the mark of liberalism at its best, the battle is not lost. The intellectual revival of liberalism is already under way in many parts of the world.

Friedrich A. Hayek, Nobel Laureate, 1966

Contents

Introduction

In 1967 I made the following observations:

Some time ago my wife and I spent a year traveling through Eastern Europe, the Middle East, and the Far East. In country after country we were deeply impressed by the striking contrast between the facts, as they appeared to us, and the ideas about the facts held by intellectuals.

Wherever we found any large element of individual freedom, some beauty in the ordinary life of the ordinary man, some measure of real progress in the material comforts at his disposal, and a live hope of further progress in the future—there we also found that the private market was the main device being used to organize economic activity. Wherever the private market was largely suppressed and the state undertook to control in detail the economic activities of its citizens (wherever, that is, detailed central economic planning reigned)—there the ordinary man was in political fetters, had a low standard of living, and was largely bereft of any conception of controlling his own destiny. The state might prosper and accomplish mighty material works. Privileged classes might enjoy a full measure of material comforts. But the ordinary man was an instrument to be used for the state's purpose, receiving no more than necessary to keep him docile and reasonably productive.

By contrast, the intellectuals everywhere took it for granted that capitalism and the market were devices for exploiting the masses, while central economic planning was the wave of the future that would set their countries on the road to rapid economic progress. I shall not soon forget the tongue-lashing I received from a prominent, highly successful, and extremely literate Indian manufacturer when I made remarks that he correctly interpreted as criticism of India's detailed central planning. Or the numerous discussions with professors at government-supported universities in India, where I was told again and again that in a country as poor as India it was essential for the government to control imports, domestic production, and the allocation of investment in order to assure that *social* priorities and not the market demand for luxuries dominated. Many of these discussions took place in comfortable university guesthouses, or relatively luxurious seminar rooms or lounges, well shielded from the nearby hovels where the common people live. One even took place in the magnificent Ashoka Hotel in New Delhi, a showplace built by the government. Yet not once was any question raised about the appropriateness of the "social priorities" reflected in the allocation of governmental funds for these amenities. ("Myths That Keep People Hungry," *Harper's,* April 1967, p. 16.)

The nearly two decades since have seen a distinct change in intellectual opinion, as it has become more and more difficult simply to ignore the facts. Intellectual opinion is no longer so monolithic as it then was in regarding central planning as the route to economic progress. Yet it is still fair to say that many if not most intellectuals remain averse to the market as an alternative mechanism; that they continue to apply a double standard in judging countries. They are reluctant to condemn countries that profess to be "socialist" or to be promoting social priorities through central planning, attributing one failure after another to mistaken application of policies rather than to the defect of the "system." In contrast, they tend to regard every shortcoming in countries regarded as "capitalist" as reflecting inherent defects of capitalism and the market, even when the shortcoming is a direct result of government interference with the market—such as the fixing of prices.

Dr. Rydenfelt's remarkable book performs an immense service in bringing together detailed evidence on the performance of fifteen widely separated countries in which the government plays a dominant role in organizing economic activity. The countries include eight Communist nations—five in the Soviet bloc plus China, Yugoslavia, and Vietnam—and seven others ranging from India and Sri Lanka in Asia to Portugal in Europe, Ghana and Tanzania in Africa, and Cuba and Argentina in Latin America.

No one who reads Dr. Rydenfelt's account of the course of events in these countries can fail to recognize the uniformity of their experience —this is at one and the same time the most fascinating feature of the book and a source of a certain amount of repetition. As each chapter unfolds, the reader is tempted to say, "I've heard that one before."

For any one country by itself, it is hard to reject a particular event —say a crop failure—as an accident due to the weather or to an avoidable mistake in planning. But when the same scenario is repeated in fourteen countries—and the one real exception, Hungary, is a state that, though ostensibly socialist, has used the market rather than central planning to organize agriculture—it is clear that something more than accident is at work.

The example of poor crops is dramatic not only because the typical excuse of poor weather is ludicrous when offered year after year and in country after country, but also, and more important, because the failure of these countries—many of which were large exporters of agricultural products before they became socialist—to produce enough food for their people has meant literal starvation for millions and real and grinding hunger for far larger numbers. But Dr. Rydenfelt's analysis covers a great deal more than agriculture. He deals with the whole of the economic activities of the nations he examines. The same contrast between "the dream and the reality," as he terms it, shows up again and again in area after area within each country and in country after country.

The detailed survey of fifteen countries, which constitutes Part II of the book, is clearly the meat in Dr. Rydenfelt's palatable sandwich. But Parts I and III are equally nutritious. The first stresses the role of the creative individual as the engine of progress, as illustrated by the American, Japanese, and German miracles—as well as by what have come to be called the Gang of Four in East Asia: Hong Kong, Singapore, Taiwan, and South Korea. It is no accident, he points out, that economic growth and prosperity have flourished precisely in those societies in which the political system promoted a sufficient measure of individual freedom to unleash the energies and ambitions of the creative entrepreneur.

In Part III Dr. Rydenfelt attributes the current "crisis" in the West to the progressive manacling of the creative entrepreneur by the state as a result of ever-higher government spending and taxes, government ownership and operation of numerous enterprises, and extensive government regulation of such private enterprises as are permitted to exist. The major hope for the future, in his view, is the widening public reaction against the expansion of government's role—a reaction that may once again release the energies of creative entrepreneurs. Dr. Rydenfelt is highly optimistic about the potential abundance that such a development could stimulate.

This highly thoughtful, original, and provocative book deserves a wide readership.

Milton Friedman
Stanford, California
January 1985

Preface

Two new philosophies—strengthening and cross-fertilizing each other —are gaining currency throughout the world: the philosophy of freedom and the philosophy of entrepreneurship.

The philosophy of freedom. In the United States the new ideas have manifested themselves as neoconservatism and neoliberalism, movements fighting for more political and economic freedom (free enterprise and free markets), movements directed not only against traditional socialism but also against the semi-socialism of public welfare. In France a related movement, the "new philosophy," directs its attacks especially against Marxism.

The philosophy of entrepreneurship. According to the new ideas, the entrepreneurs hold a key position in society. Only a few individuals are endowed with entrepreneurial talents, but for these few to utilize their talents to originate and develop enterprises and produce growth, wealth, and employment—they must be offered an economic environment with adequate incentives.

The new ideas of the philosophies of freedom and entrepreneurship are revolutionary in the true sense of the word and will everywhere fundamentally transform the societies in which they work. That these ideas under such circumstances should be seen as dangerous and shocking by all representatives of vested interests and defenders of existing systems was to be expected. That the ideas, nonetheless, have been able to steal into the camps of polar enemies, the conservatives and the socialists, and deeply affect their thinking, bears witness to their penetrative powers.

In the United States and Great Britain, for instance, the new ideas dominate the present governments. The time is evidently ripe for them. Why? Let us point to some of the causes:

The bankruptcy of socialism throughout the world is a primary cause. In its own camps the fires of socialism are dying, its dreams and visions fading.

Ideas of public welfare in so-called welfare states have been seriously discredited during recent years. These semi-socialist systems have been developing into bureaucratic dinosaurs that produce less and less services—at more and more prohibitive costs—to the consumers.

The value of entrepreneurs during the last trying years of crisis has come to be understood by more and more people. At long last entrepreneurs are being regarded as a unique resource to be fostered and encouraged—not for the sake of the entrepreneurs but for the sake of the people, who desperately demand more production and more employment.

Established economists and politicians have—as in the 1930s—proved to be quite impotent doctors, able neither to explain the present crisis nor to prescribe efficient cures against it. Keynesian solutions, despite enormous doses and gigantic costs, have been a total failure. In the present confusion the new ideas are able not only to explain the roots of the present crisis but to prescribe efficient cures, too.

After a decade of crisis when, despite enormously expensive governmental cures, mass unemployment occurred, a general pessimism developed. The crisis was seen as a chronic malady, and unemployment as the outcome of fundamental structural changes—a "technological" unemployment bound to increase continuously. The groups in power responsible for the crisis were, of course, eager to promote the analogy: they behaved like doctors who, having failed to heal the patient, hasten to declare the disease to be chronic and beyond help. In the darkness of this pessimism the new ideas emerged as a beacon of optimism.

From the modern science of ecology we have learned about our dependence on our physical environment and about dangers that threaten to pollute and destroy it. We ought to learn, too, that people are equally dependent on their economic and social environments, and that they will develop their full potentials only in favorable environments with adequate incentives. From studies of creativity we have learned that individuals are endowed with creative powers of different kinds, and never is man more happy than when allowed to develop his full creative potentials. And from hard experience we learn, moreover, that full potentials are possible only in environments of freedom. If by regulation and force you deny a man his freedom, you kill his incentive to create and produce, reduce the satisfaction he derives from his work, and impair his quality of life.

Granting a man freedom and enabling him to fully develop his creative potentials not only improves the quality of his life, but encourages, as a secondary effect, a higher production. Whoever destroys the productive environment of others poisons the spring from which he himself must drink.

During my lifetime, I have listened to and benefited from many teachers. In producing this book I feel especially indebted to three of them: Milton and Rose Friedman, my teachers in the philosophy of freedom, and Israel Kirzner, my teacher in the philosophy of entrepreneurship.

Sven Rydenfelt, Lund University, Sweden, 1984

PART I

The Importance of the Entrepreneurial Environment

It is by now fairly well recognized that standard economic theory has developed along lines that virtually exclude the entrepreneurial role. . . . Our discussion has focused attention on a neglected aspect of economic decision-making, the urgency for incentives for the "entrepreneurial" discovery of what opportunities exist for economic action. . . . A great deal of work is waiting to be done in the economics of entrepreneurship.

Israel M. Kirzner, 1980

PART 1

The Importance of the
Entrepreneurial Environment

Chapter 1

A General Theory of Incentives

> A hundred men who will are stronger than a hundred thousand who shall.
>
> *Arthur Schopenhauer,* 1819

The Industrial Revolution—An Economic Miracle

> Both agricultural development and industrialization proceed because a certain environment has arisen which is conducive to human creativity. The real seed is the release of human abilities. The initial capital is human and not material.
>
> *Ronald C. Nairn,* American agricultural expert, 1979

The industrial revolution, according to common interpretation, began in Britain at the end of the eighteenth century. In school we learn that it was brought about by such fantastic new contraptions as steam engines, spinning machines, and mechanical looms, invented and put to use about 1770.

That account, however, is superficial and raises questions. Why was this inventiveness and creativity released during the eighteenth century? Why not in the thirteenth century or the sixteenth? And why not in France? Or Holland? Or China? The Swedish economist and historian Eli F. Heckscher gives the following answer:

The difference was not due to the fact that England had been the industrial pioneer, since France had been more of a pioneer than England during the 17th century. Neither was it due—at least not primarily—to the fact that England had coal and iron ore, since the most fundamental revolution was in the cotton industry. Not a single pound of raw cotton was produced in England.

Neither was the cause a greater interest in industrial techniques in England than in France—rather the opposite was true. In [France] a stream of State regulations with hundreds of legal paragraphs were issued to control the various branches of industry, especially the textile industry; it was a stream unequaled in England. A whole hierarchy of civil servants was created in France to supervise the observance of the regulations. The French guilds were engaged in the same task, while England scarcely had any civil servants designated for this, or indeed, for any other duties. The French penalties were severe. Measures against the illegal import of printed calicoes, for instance, may have cost 16,000 lives; certainly the number that was made galley slaves for illegal importation was much greater than that.

And so these very measures prevented French trade and industries from utilizing any number of possibilities that were beginning to present themselves. In other words, government regulation [in France] froze the existing state of affairs.[1]

During the preindustrial period, the entrepreneurs in handicrafts and trade were so closely allied with the groups in power—the kings and the nobility—that they could use the state's coercion apparatus to grant themselves privileges of various kinds—monopolies, establishment controls, customs, and other obstacles to the import of competing goods. Guilds and mercantilism proved counterproductive—industries were paralyzed and development was prevented.

Criticism of these regulatory systems during the eighteenth century —from Adam Smith and many others—grew, however, and even before reforms were introduced, the restrictive practices were undermined. Decisive appears to have been the fact that the manufacturing industry and its factories were innovations not covered by the regulations that governed handicrafts and trade.

Manufacturing was thus able to develop in a sort of no-man's-land, a regulatory vacuum, which meant almost unlimited economic freedom for the entrepreneurs. Suddenly a field opened to provide the very ecological environment in which private enterprise could develop and flourish. Thus it was demonstrated that many people have latent entrepreneurial talents that cannot develop until they encounter the right soil and climate.

From the end of the eighteenth century until the middle of the nineteenth, Britain was the scene of an explosion of industrial enterprise, an economic expansion unequaled in history. It was as if a dam had been opened. The absence of economic restrictions and controls in combination with unlimited possibilities for profit stimulated capable and inventive people to set up a continuous stream of enterprise.

The industrial revolution in Britain remains the most remarkable of all economic miracles. A new age, the age of industrialism, was born, and its pioneers and leaders, the entrepreneurs, formed the broad front of an offensive that would roll across national boundaries until at last it conquered the world.

The new technology of steam engines and textile machines did not arise accidentally. If there is one thing that present-day scientists are agreed upon, it is that inventive talent must enjoy freedom in order to develop its innate possibilities. During the period of the industrial revolution the inventors could work in freedom, and free enterpreneurs were prepared to buy and use the new machines.

And, beyond any doubt, the inventors created remarkable things. One worker with a spinning machine could produce as much thread as two hundred manual workers—just one example of the enormous increase in productivity made possible by the new techniques. The development that began in the textile industry soon spread to other branches of industry. Heckscher described the miraculous effects of the industrial revolution in England as follows:

> Within 50 years, from 1781 to 1833, the use of raw cotton—and thereby the cotton industry—increased by 48 times in England. During the subsequent period from the 1820s to 1913 this figure increased "only" by 29 times, but the production of pig-iron increased by 48 times and the production of coal by 77 times.[2]

The British historian and chief editor of *The New Statesman*, Paul Johnson, wrote:

> Prior to the eighteenth century it was rare for even the most advanced economies, those of England and Holland, to achieve one percent growth in any year. Beginning in the 1780s, England

achieved a then-unprecedented annual growth rate of two percent. By the end of the decade a rate of four percent had been attained —a rate which was to be sustained for the next 50 years.

During the nineteenth century Britain increased the size of its work force by 400 percent. Real wages doubled during the period 1800–1850, and doubled again from 1850 to 1900. This meant there was a 1600 percent increase in the production and consumption of wage goods during the century. Nothing like this had happened anywhere before in the whole of history.[3]

The Agrarian Revolution—An Economic Miracle

> What a society performs does not depend on arms or subsidies or on physical natural resources. It depends on the culture of the people and, above all, on the political system.
>
> *P. T. Bauer,* British economist, 1980

Environment and motivation explain, among other things, how powers that have been bound up can be released and how the creative forces behind the industrial revolution in England were liberated when the old restrictive practices of the feudal society, with its guilds and mercantilism, were eliminated. In Sweden, as elsewhere, the industrial revolution was preceded by an agrarian revolution, another release of bound-up forces, which converted the old low-producing Swedish agriculture into one of the most efficient in the world. In the beginning of the nineteenth century Sweden was a backward country in an obscure corner of Europe. Of its population 90 percent were engaged in agriculture, an occupational distribution found today only in the most underdeveloped countries. Several more decades would pass before the tide of the industrial revolution reached the shores of Sweden.

Between 1760 and 1814 the old English collective agricultural system was replaced by a system that gave peasants rights of ownership of their land. This agricultural revolution in England was called the enclosure movement.

In Sweden the same revolution began with successive redistributional land reforms, paving the way for a system of private farms at the beginning of the nineteenth century. These reforms broke down a rigid village system which had conserved the old methods and had prevented change and development.

The old village system, under which widely scattered plots of land had been cultivated collectively, had paralyzed the Swedish countryside. Everyone in the village had been forced to follow the will of the conservative majority (the majority is always conservative) and adapt to the old patterns, sowing and harvesting simultaneously, in accordance with ancient tested methods. The land reforms broke down the old village system and liberated the individual farmer, thereby putting an end to an old form of collective agriculture. New paths in industry, as in all other forms of human life, are always blazed by individuals—thinkers and creators who test new techniques and new forms of production. When the collective system was eliminated, people whose creative powers had been constrained could begin to experiment with new methods of cultivation. When the pioneers were successful, the conservative masses soon followed them, and winds of change began to blow over the Swedish countryside. Before the redistributional land reforms, all noncultivated land—pastures, forests, and so on—were owned jointly by the villagers. This system functioned as a barrier to the opening up of new land, since the group was unwilling to release jointly owned land for cultivation by individuals. An element of this unwillingness, to be sure, was jealousy of the more energetic and capable colleagues and neighbors. When the land reform went into effect, every peasant received his own farm as a single unit to cultivate as he saw fit. Release from the collective bonds meant a release of creative powers, the driving force behind the agrarian revolution.

New methods of cultivation and the breeding of new and better animals and plants were important ingredients of the revolution. Another was the extensive opening up of new land to cultivation.

According to the most recent calculations, the cultivated land area in Sweden increased from some 1,500,000 hectares in 1805 to 3,200,000 hectares in 1865.[4]

Although the greatly increased production of foodstuffs led to a population explosion, the increase in cultivated land area during these sixty years was 113 percent, while the increase in population was only 70 percent.

As an illustration of the expansion of cultivated land, only 15 percent of the area of Skane, Sweden's southernmost province and its granary, was under cultivation before 1805, whereas 50 percent had come under cultivation about a hundred years later.

In the beginning of the 1980s the approximately 3 to 4 percent of the total Swedish labor force that was employed in agriculture produced more food than could be consumed within the country, an accomplishment that placed Swedish farmers, alongside those of the United States, among the most productive in the world.

The American Economic Miracle

A wise and frugal government, which shall restrain men from injuring one another, which shall leave them otherwise free to regulate their own pursuits of industry and improvement, and which shall not take from the mouth of labor the bread it has earned, is the sum of good government.

Thomas Jefferson, first inaugural address, 1801

The English colonies in America won their national independence in 1783, and something of a Golden Age followed for the United States, a legendary period of economic freedom and a market economy. Nowhere else in history is it possible to find a period of such unlimited economic liberty and optimum entrepreneurial environment. In this new nation there was no royalty, state church, or state bureaucracy—the traditional institutions of oppression—and people who had fled from oppression and exploitation in Europe vigorously fought every attempt to establish similar institutions in the new country.

Freedom from economic bonds released entrepreneurial activities of such strength and over such a long period as to surpass anything previously experienced. The demand for labor became so great that domestic resources were quite insufficient. Between 1820 and 1970—a century and a half—some 44 million immigrants found a national home, employment, and a livelihood in the United States.

The U.S.A., with a population only a fraction of England's at the beginning of the war of independence in 1775, grew so rapidly that by the middle of the nineteenth century it had surpassed the mother country in population, and before the end of the century it had also surpassed it in economic prosperity. After World War I it became evident that the United States had assumed England's earlier position as the leading political and economic power of the world.

During the two centuries between 1775 and 1975 the population of France doubled, while that of Sweden increased four times and that of Great Britain six times. During the same period that of the United States increased 68 times—a population explosion unprecedented in history.

The miracle of this development is not that a high birth rate and unlimited immigration led to a population explosion, but that private enterprise, liberated from its bonds, could create jobs for all these people, jobs that paid the highest wages in the world.

Here I give the American miracle an entrepreneurial and ecological explanation. Earlier analysts most often attributed it to natural resources and material circumstances. They stressed that from the beginning there was almost unlimited access to virgin land, and endless plains waiting for the plow. But, during that time, enormous areas suitable for cultivation and agriculture existed throughout the world where no expansion was triggered.

According to another common explanation, the enormous assets of unexploited natural resources—agricultural land, forests, ores, coal, and oil—made this development possible. A systematic study of rich and poor countries, however, reveals that the materialistic approach is inadequate to explain prosperity or underdevelopment. Poor countries—India, Indonesia, and China—may actually be rich in natural resources, while some of the wealthiest countries—Denmark, the Netherlands, Switzerland, New Zealand, and Japan—may be almost totally lacking in such resources.

The Japanese Economic Miracle

The outstanding examples of economic development have occurred precisely when there has not been a policy for increased savings, but when there has been an incentive for people to save and invest. As a matter for description, development is a process in which there are widespread incentives to individual people to do something to promote production in the future rather than simply to consume in the present.

Milton Friedman, 1968

One of the most remarkable economic miracles in history was launched in Japan in 1868 by the so-called Meiji restoration. During the following two or three decades Japan was converted from an economically weak and backward feudal society to a modern state on the Western model.

Having suffered humiliations at the hands of several European countries, the leaders of the restoration in Japan realized that an industrial development following the Western pattern was the only way to prevent any of the old world powers from incorporating Japan into their empires. The most rapid industrialization possible would create a stable enough economic base to support strong military forces for defense.

Through a comprehensive land reform, serfs became free peasants and began to modernize a backward agricultural system. Simultaneously, other reforms brought free enterprise and opened the gates to an industrial revolution of the same type that had come about a hundred years earlier in England. Economic freedom created the environment and soil in which latent entrepreneurial talents could germinate and develop, and new enterprises sprang up like mushrooms after the rain.

Modern military forces were built up, and the victory over the Russian Empire in 1905 confirmed the country's newly won economic and military might.

Defeat in World War II put an end to earlier nationalistic dreams of military victories and conquests. Conditions in Japan at the end of the war were described by the former American ambassador to Japan, Edwin O. Reischauer, as follows:

> The war left Japan a thoroughly devastated and demoralized land . . . Approximately half of the urban housing of Japan had been burned to the ground by American air raids. Tokyo's population had shrunk by more than a half, Osaka's by almost two-thirds. With the destruction of the cities and the virtual disappearance of the merchant marine, which had maintained the flow of Japan's economic lifeblood, industrial production had plummeted, standing in 1946 at a mere seventh of the 1941 figure. The people were clothed in rags, ill-fed, and both physically and emotionally exhausted.[5]

The American forces of occupation weeded out about 200,000 of those who had been responsible for wartime military policy, thereby paralyzing the state bureaucracy and weakening the central authorities. As adherents of economic freedom and a market economy, the Americans sought during the occupation, which lasted until 1952, to favor a free enterprise system. The Japanese were willing learners and continued to pursue an economic policy that embodied great freedom for private enterprise. The increases in production between 1955 and 1970 well deserve to be called a miracle. By 1955 Japan ranked thirtieth in gross national product (GNP) among the industrial countries of the world. In 1968, thirteen years later, Japan had advanced to second place among the Western industrial countries, immediately after the United States. Despite temporary reverses, Japanese economic progress continued even during the "sick" 1970s and is still going on during the 1980s.

Since the Meiji restoration, the Japanese government has had much to do with industry, and the question has often been asked whether Japanese enterprise has really been free. Contrary to the situation in the Western welfare states, however, the Japanese government has tried to facilitate development by assisting private enterprise—not by forcing it into a straitjacket of state regulations.

Without an entrepreneurial environment of a sort that has stimulated the creativity and initiative of the Japanese, the miracle would be inexplicable. Two economists, Chiaki Nishiyama of Tokyo and G. C. Allen of London, have offered the following observation:

> Far from possessing a monolithic economy with the bureaucracy in control, Japan provides a superb example of the free enterprise system. Her success is a splendid vindication of that system.
>
> Private enterprise has probably had more scope in Japan than in most other countries since the war. The size of the public sector in relation to the economy as a whole is only about half that in most Western countries. Many industries which in Europe are usually found in public ownership fall into the private sector in Japan; this applies to the electricity generating and the steel industries.[6]

So far I have emphasized the importance of offering entrepreneurs an environment that liberates and stimulates their creative powers and initiative. The same need exists, of course, among all producers, including the employees in a firm; an environment that liberates and stimulates their creativity and initiative has a tremendous effect on their productivity.

The environment of the employees is undoubtedly one of the weak points in Western industry. A Japanese economist, Masaki Imai, has described the situation as follows:

> While in many Western countries there are a handful of hardworking, highly competitive and ambitious executives, there are also a good number of less motivated workers who make up the bulk of the working class. There, the distinction between the manager and the managed is clear and there can be no misunderstanding.

The former manages and hopes to motivate the latter. In Japan, the manager and the managed are one and the same.[7]

Japanese managers seem to be far more aware of the importance of creating environments that will motivate their employees than their colleagues in the West. The top managers in Japan devote most of their time and energy to the task of creating good human relations within the company, delegating economic and technical tasks to their assistants. One of Japan's foremost experts on this subject, Chie Nakane, characterizes Japanese managers in these words:

> Some American executives visiting Japan have expressed surprise that so many Japanese directors are unable to explain the details of their own enterprise. They rely cheerfully on their beloved and trusted subordinates to run the business; of much greater concern to them is the maintenance of happy relations among the men, for in this they believe lies the key to business success.
>
> There is a high degree of personal involvement between manager and employee. It is customary for the director or department head to attend the employee's wedding ceremony as a go-between. Indeed, a director spends considerable time away from his office on such occasions.
>
> It is my conviction that in Japanese society, at least at present, this type of personal relations is the group's driving force and brings greater success than any other type of group organization.[8]

Japanese managers realize that their most important task is to win the affection and friendship of their employees and that such things cannot be bought for money, not for wages, no matter how high they may be. The employee's presence in the work place and certain acts that he performs can be bought, but his enthusiasm, initiative, and loyalty, his desire to do his best, cannot be bought. Still more is it impossible to produce these attitudes by means of threats and force. These qualities must be won, and the difference between winning and forcing is, in a deeper sense, the difference between democracy and dictatorship.

In my book about Japan I analyze the environmental basis of the Japanese economic miracle in the following way:

> The pleasure of working is a quality of life, one of the greatest gifts that can be offered human beings in a short life. Whoever offers this quality to a fellow man is richly rewarded, not only with good work but also with gratitude and friendship. To deny a worker satisfac-

tion is worse than a crime. It is stupidity, harming not only the worker, but the administrator as well. In our ignorance we believe that lack of satisfaction in and enthusiasm for our work is in accordance with the natural order.[9]

The German Economic Miracle

There was no miracle. It was the consistently applied social market economy and nothing else that quickly eliminated the chaos in trade and industry.

Ludwig Erhard, German Minister of Finance, 1953

Manufacturing gains

One of the most conspicuous economic miracles of the twentieth century developed in West Germany some years after World War II. Even there it was possible for an environment of economic freedom to be created, an environment that released an explosion of entrepreneurship. One cause was the comprehensive denazification process, the simple removal of the bureaucratic apparatus. The administrative organs of central control were more or less paralyzed.

The situation was therefore highly favorable for such a coup as that carried out in June 1948 by the later Minister of Finance Ludwig Erhard. Price controls and rationing were rescinded with the stroke of a pen, a currency reform was effected, and Erhard's "social market economy" was established.

West German entrepreneurs, formerly shackled by central regulations, could shake off their bonds and begin an economic expansion such as no one at that time had dared to imagine. Once they had regained their freedom, nothing could stop them, neither bombed-out factories and installations nor the fact that machinery and equipment had been confiscated by the victorious powers. A manufacturing industry whose volume of production during the first six months of 1948 had measured 50 percent of its 1939 volume, achieved 130 percent of that 1939 volume, only three years later. And despite the fact that 8 million refugees flowed into West Germany between 1945 and 1950 with more to follow later, it was possible to reduce unemployment from 10 percent of the labor force in 1950 to 1 percent in 1960, while the number of workers increased from 14 to 21 million.

During the same decade the West German share of world exports increased from 10 percent to 25 percent. In that period, Britain's share decreased from 35 percent to 24 percent. This eruption of enterprise produced a demand for labor so urgent that the domestic force, including refugees, was insufficient to meet it. By the end of the 1950s, therefore, a stream of foreign job-seekers began to flow into West Germany, a stream that increased rapidly during the 1960s. In 1983 there were still 4.5 million foreign workers, of whom 1.6 million were Turks.

The German example dramatically demonstrates the capacity of private enterprise to create new and more employment when it is offered an optimal entrepreneurial environment. It is an example worth pondering during present economic crises.

To put it simply, the environment was altered in such a way that entrepreneurial talents could be released and activated. Of course, more traditional explanations have been put forward. One of these asserts that confiscation of the West German industrial machines by the British, French, and Russian victors caused the Germans to fill the gap with new, up-to-date machines, while for many years the victors had to be satisfied with the old. The fact is that, lacking capital, the Germans had for several years to get on with old machines discarded by the victors.

Similarly, an enormous postwar influx of refugees, educated, trained adult workers, has been pointed to as the injection that triggered the miracle. But surely in any other country, an influx of refugees equal to 25 percent of the original population would be a burden and not an asset.

Finally, it has been claimed that Marshall Plan aid from the United States provided the capital that fueled the expansion. Total American aid between 1945 and 1953 amounted to $3.5 billion, of which approximately half was Marshall Plan aid. While this was welcome assistance to a devastated nation, it is in fact a small figure beside the total investment made after the Erhard coup in 1949. The Marshall Plan aid does not explain the miracle.

And it should not be forgotten that until 1948 analyses in newspapers, magazines, books, and reports predicted a dark economic future for West Germany. Not a single expert would claim that the confiscation of machinery or the influx of refugees was anything but a terrible burden, rendering economic recovery infinitely more difficult. Common opinion had it that West Germany would continue to be a burden to the rest of Europe throughout the foreseeable future.

Farmers, Food Supply, and Incentives

> The people in question here—the farmers—are presumed to be stupid cattle who can be milked by their sophisticated masters in the cities. But they are not so stupid. Sooner or later they react by producing less.
>
> *Harry G. Johnson,* British economist, 1971

In all poor countries, peasants constitute up to 90 percent of the population. But they are scattered over large areas, and this makes it difficult for them to cooperate and to defend themselves against oppression and exploitation.

It is, in fact, only in capitalist countries that farmers have been able to function as free entrepreneurs and demonstrate the miraculous production volumes of which they are capable. In the United States, for example, only 3 to 4 percent of the population is engaged in agriculture, but American farmers manage to feed the entire population and produce substantial quantities for export.

The British economist Michael Lipton asserts that the basic cause of stagnation and poverty in underdeveloped countries is usually to be found in governmental oppression and exploitation of the peasants by means of policies imposed to supply the industrial and urban populations with cheap food. With few exceptions the regimes in these poor countries pursue socialist policies.[10]

Similarly, economist Theodore Schultz ascribes responsibility for agricultural stagnation in poor countries to price controls. Excessively low prices have deprived peasants of the income and capital that would have enabled them to invest and modernize as farmers in the West have been able to do.[11]

In these countries the political leaders are generally so intent on developing manufacturing industries that they seem to forget that agriculture is the basic industry, the foundation on which all society must rest. In all socialist countries the peasantry, a remnant of capitalism, is treated as an outgroup, whose sole task is to produce cheap food for the ingroups in the cities; the status of the farmer in socialist states, in fact, corresponds to that of the serfs under feudalism.

Many great countries that are now socialist once produced large food surpluses for export; ironically, they must now satisfy more and more of their needs with imports from capitalist countries. Their continuously increasing dependence on imports demonstrates how quickly an incentive-killing agricultural policy can convert a plus into a minus, a surplus into a deficit, a granary into a hunger area.

All peasants, even the illiterates in the most backward countries, understand perfectly well that if they mistreat and starve their livestock, output will be poor. Why should not the well-educated leaders in socialist countries comprehend that if they mistreat and starve their peasants, food production will suffer?[12]

With these economic weaknesses, however, another failure must be counted. The prophets of the socialist gospel have always promised to redeem the world from oppression and exploitation and to celebrate the weakest and poorest members of society. In all socialist countries the peasants constitute the poorest and weakest group. Study and analysis of agriculture and agricultural policies in a large number of socialist countries make it clear that a gulf exists between theory and practice, between promise and fulfillment. Socialists in power have systematically favored the strong, well-situated urban groups—industrial workers, police, soldiers, and bureaucrats, the political supporters of the regime— while, just as systematically, they have oppressed and plundered the peasants.

Overpopulation and World Starvation

The recent rapid increase in population in less developed countries reflects a steep fall in mortality. This development represents substantial improvement in conditions, since people value a longer life.

P. T. Bauer, British economist, 1981

If a food shortage develops in a given country, it is natural to conclude that that country's food supply is inadequate. But the problem could be seen otherwise: it might be concluded that the population is too large. This latter interpretation is the one preferred by political leaders in many countries with food shortages.

To those who would subscribe to this interpretation, the cause of the shortage is an excessively high birth rate—a population explosion—and the remedy is family planning. The responsibility for the food shortage is thereby quickly and conveniently attributed to the victims of the shortage.

Even if family planning measures are desirable, this interpretation has all too often been used as an out for the politicians. In countries that maintain production incentives, the peasants, in fact, have proved able to satisfy the food demands, even in countries where population density is high—as it is, for example, in the Netherlands and Taiwan.

In a special issue of *Scientific American* the question of potential world production of food and textile fibers was raised, and it was concluded that a volume twelve times as great as that presently produced is possible. It was found that the world's peasantry, if offered favorable incentives, would be able to feed and clothe 40 billion people—ten times the present world population.[13]

In the popular debate about the threat of starvation in the world's 140 underdeveloped countries—where socialist policies are most often pursued—wild increases in population are generally cited as the cause. The conclusion is that family planning is the logical remedy. A far greater threat, however, is a parasitic and stifling agricultural policy.

The socialist countries of the world are, as a rule, unable to feed their own people. An economic-political system with such a fundamental deficiency must be inefficient and, in the long run, dangerous.[14]

The Miracle Drug of Borrowing

> Nations sink deeper and deeper into an immense ocean of debt. Public debt, initially a security for governments . . . when resorted to excessively, will most probably bring disaster.
>
> *Edmund Burke,* 1790

Politicians delight in granting privileges and subsidies to their constituents. In exchange, of course, they count on getting the votes of the privileged. The greatest anxiety of politicians is that they may be forced to reject their constituents' demands because of inadequate resources.

By borrowing, that rejection can be spared. Like a miracle drug promising instant results, borrowing allays the anxiety and postpones the problem into a distant future.

But growing debts mean growing debt-service burdens, burdens that can conveniently be met for many years by means of new credits. A continuously increasing proportion of the new loans is consumed by interest on the old ones. The borrowing machine requires more and more fuel, and a condition for keeping the machine going is ever-larger new loans.

Borrowing, especially foreign borrowing, is like an oil well—sooner or later it dries up. The credit potential of nations, like that of private individuals, is limited, and a mountain of accumulated debt is bound to collapse.

We have seen the consequences of foreign borrowing in problems of recent years. By 1984 some fifty countries reached the end of the credit road and were bankrupt. There are fundamental distinctions, however, between bankrupt individuals and bankrupt countries. While the private properties of a bankrupt individual can be confiscated by creditors, no corresponding confiscation of the assets of a bankrupt country can be made.

Every year more and more countries go bankrupt, and, with few exceptions, they will probably never repay their debts to other countries. Doubtless many of them would be able to repay, but since payments mean severe privation and no creditors can force them to pay, most of them will prefer to postpone payments into a distant and hazy future.

Their debts virtually remitted, they may breathe more easily, but the hefty price they must pay for their failure as borrowers is expulsion from the credit markets of the world. No matter how urgent their need for more capital, the doors of the creditors will be closed. Institutions such as the International Monetary Fund (IMF) and the World Bank sometimes grant obviously bankrupt countries new credits. In fact, such credits are aid more than they are loans.

Borrowing countries live far beyond their means. They use—and abuse—foreign credits as addicts use narcotics, and the habit brings only a fool's paradise. Sooner or later the doses will stop and severe withdrawal pains will follow. Both production and consumption in such countries will have become adapted to a continuous net supply of capital from abroad, a supply that has enabled large import surpluses. When the foreign-capital flow stops, there can only be drastic reductions in the volume of imports—in the flow of fuels, raw materials, machines, and spare parts to industry. Chain reactions with severe consequences follow.

The bankruptcies of recent years have meant gigantic losses for the creditor countries. Why weren't they foreseen, and why wasn't the credit flow stopped? One significant reason was the serious economic crisis in the Western world during the 1970s. Economies stagnated, the ordinary export markets shrank, and rapidly growing volumes of unemployment forced the crisis countries to seek new markets for exports. To create employment, new markets had to be opened up. Exports to such markets, however, had to be bought at the price of reduced security requirements in lending. If private corporations hesitated, they were often assuaged by state credit guarantees. As time wore on, lenders were unwilling to prick the credit bubble and take the consequences. By granting new credits they postponed the threats and bought themselves respite. If declarations of default had been issued, the lenders would have been forced to write off claims and report losses so large that the stability of the banking community would have been undermined.[15]

The Role of the Entrepreneur

I will maintain that, despite a number of highly perceptive contributions, the proper role of the entrepreneur in the market system is not typically presented in its true light, or with adequate recognition for its being the driving force for the entire market process.

Israel M. Kirzner, 1973

Unemployment in the 1970s and 1980s is a social malady that has proven quite resilient against attempts at remedy and cure. Despite energetic and costly measures, it has continued to spread; in many industrial countries it has spread so extensively that, as in the 1930s, it can only be described as mass unemployment.

To the very last our economic doctors have believed in the theories of Keynes, according to which unemployment results from a deficiency in the total demand of a society. In a Keynesian world the government's task is to cure unemployment by radically increasing that total demand, and the process is financed by borrowing. But despite the fact that in the last decade governmental deficit financing has increased successively in many countries—to an extent Keynes would never have imagined—the malady has only been aggravated. Today it is the secondary effects of these overdoses that seriously threaten the patients. Lately, analysts have come to conclude that new cures, new medicines are necessary; that the old Keynesian prescriptions from the 1930s cannot do in the 1980s. We need a new Keynes, and we are looking for one among our economists. Alas, today's economists are as divided and as much at a loss as those who struggled with the mass unemployment problems of the 1930s.

The fundamental thesis of this book is that the roots and causes of present economic ills such as unemployment have been discovered, and that a cure is available. The answer is in the "theory of entrepreneurship."

The new theory of entrepreneurship has fundamental implications for the theory of growth. According to neoclassical production theories, the underdevelopment of the poor countries is primarily due to lack of capital, while according to the new theory of entrepreneurship, the supply of entrepreneurial incentives is more essential than the supply of capital. Experiences in different periods of history as well as in different places—in industrial revolutions above all—prove that entrepreneurs are able to create capital if left to themselves.

As in all scientific research work, many people have contributed to the new theories of entrepreneurship. One of the early fathers of the theory was the French economist J. B. Say (1767–1832), who, besides being a pioneer for present-day supply-side economics, demonstrated deep insights in the dynamics of production and growth by adding a fourth factor of production to the classic triad of land, labor, and capital —namely the entrepreneur. The Austrian-American economist Joseph A. Schumpeter (1883–1950), another of the fathers of the theory, discussed the dynamics of production similarly:

> The entrepreneurial activity of the leader, which is indeed a necessary condition of the realization of the [new] combination, may be conceived as a means of production. . . . In most cases, as we have said, the means of production are replaceable, but not the leader.[16]

Schumpeter emphasized the dynamic role of the entrepreneur as distinguished from the static role of the manager. One of the major shortcomings of the classical economists was, according to Schumpeter, their lack of appreciation for the entrepreneur's role.

> Ricardo, the Ricardians, and also Senior . . . in fact almost accomplished what I have described as an impossible feat, namely, the exclusion of the figure of the entrepreneur completely. For them—as well as for Marx—the business process runs substantially by itself, the one thing needful to make it run being an adequate supply of capital.[17]

The same accusation could, to be sure, be directed against most economists of today. The approach of our traditional economic theory to production continues to be a "mechanical" one. In one of our most widely used university textbooks the following formulation is found:

> Production is roughly like a sausage machine. Certain elements, such as raw materials and the services of capital and labor, are fed in at one end, and a product emerges at the other. The materials and factor services used in the production process are called *inputs,* and the products that emerge are called *outputs.*[18]

Such theories take little account of the entrepreneur, while the more humanistic new theory insists that the entrepreneur and the supply of incentives occupy a central position.

The new theory of entrepreneurship has deep roots in the Austrian school of economists, a school experiencing a revival in recent years. A fundamental idea of one of its most prominent members, F. A. Hayek —Nobel Laureate in 1974—is that economic realities are sufficiently complex to make our knowledge of them bound to be limited. Because of these inevitable limitations, our opportunities for intervening in the market and directing economic development also are limited. Very often the results of intervention will be quite other than the results aimed for:

> If a man is not to do more harm than good in his efforts to improve the social order, he will have to learn that in this, as in all other fields where essentially complexity of an organized kind prevails, he cannot acquire the full knowledge which would make mastery of the events possible. He will therefore have to use what knowledge he

can achieve, not to shape the results as the craftsman shapes his handiwork, but rather to cultivate a growth by providing the appropriate environment, in the manner in which the gardener does this for his plants.[19]

Supporters of the new theory of entrepreneurship as well as the Austrian school hold that free markets with free prices, free competition, and free trade are the ideal environment for entrepreneurial activities. Governments by means of state regulations and restrictions can greatly impair this environment, but if they choose to eliminate regulations, can greatly improve it. During the last few decades governments in the East as well as in the West have pursued policies that seriously impair the entrepreneurial environment, and economic crises have been the result. The governments seem to be unconscious of causes and effects, unconscious of the tie between policy and crisis.

Well aware of the importance of politics to the ecology of a nation's economy, Ludwig von Mises (1881–1973), one of the fathers of the Austrian school, wrote as early as 1949:

> The entrepreneur is also jeopardized by political dangers. Government policies, revolutions, and wars can damage or annihilate his enterprise. Such events do not affect him alone; they affect the market economy as such and all individuals, although not all of them to the same extent. . . . Policies hostile to capitalism may deprive the consumers of the greater part of the benefits they would have reaped from unhampered entrepreneurial activities.[20]

There are those who will react negatively when confronted with these ideas, suspecting the new theory of entrepreneurship to be a new ideology launched and sponsored by businessmen in order to make themselves a privileged class. These people are wrong. According to the fundamental thesis of the new theory, majorities in power during the last ten or fifteen years have pursued policies of oppression and exploitation of the entrepreneurial minority: oppression by means of innumerable state regulations, and exploitation by means of confiscatory taxes and fees. Such policies have meant a systematic disruption of the entrepreneurial environment and an effective killing of incentive. The inevitable consequence has been ongoing economic crisis, stagnation, and unemployment.

Countries like the United States and Sweden today can boast the best educated, healthiest, and most skillful labor force in the world. But what is the use of these assets and resources if we continue to manacle our entrepreneurs and thereby paralyze the very creators of growth, wealth, and employment?

PART II

Crises and Entrepreneurship in the East

> The peasants have been the big stumbling-block for all Socialist revolutions, the unsolved problem of Marxist theory.
>
> *Arthur Koestler,* 1969

Chapter 2

The Soviet Union

> A phase has come to an end. The driving force that had its origin in the October Revolution has exhausted itself. We must present a new socialism based on freedom and democracy.
>
> *Enrico Berlinguer,* Chairman of the Italian Communist Party, 1982

Lenin's Terror against the Peasants

> If we do not apply terror and immediate executions, we will get nowhere. It is better that a hundred innocent are killed than that one guilty person escapes.
>
> *V. I. Lenin,* 1918

According to such socialist pioneers as Marx, Engels, and Kautsky, those who had been private peasants under capitalism were doomed in countries in which socialists had assumed power. Development, Engels declared, would run over these peasants in the same way as a locomotive runs over a wheelbarrow. An opposing opinion was presented by the German social democrat Eduard Bernstein (1850–1932), who considered small farms to be the most rational form of agricultural enterprises.

As a genuine city dweller, Marx was obsessed by a deep-seated contempt for peasants and the countryside. In the *Communist Manifesto* he wrote about the "rural idiocy."[1] One explanation of Marx's contempt for capitalist agriculture, with its countless small farms, was his gigantomania, his uncritical faith in the superior efficiency of big enterprise. When the Communists under Lenin's leadership seized power in Russia in 1917, they looked upon the private businessmen and peasants of that time as capitalist profiteers and class enemies. In accordance with their socialist doctrines, they introduced a command economy, in which the activities and production of businessmen and peasants would be entirely controlled by decrees of the new masters.

To frighten people into subservience and obedience, the new regime had at its disposal the state coercion apparatus—police, soldiers, prisons, and executioners—which it had taken over from the old regime, an apparatus that they expanded and supplemented with political commissars and slave camps.[2] Since both industrial products and foodstuffs were needed, the businessmen and peasants were ordered to continue production—in reality as feudal serfs under the new masters.

All profits were to be eliminated in a state in which the masters, in their mercy, granted the serfs the means of subsistence necessary to maintain their working capacity. In reality the serfs were treated worse than livestock. Even if a peasant saw his domestic animals only as means of production, he usually took care of them and treated them well. If the new masters had regarded their serfs as a means of production, they would have treated them like livestock. But they regarded them as class enemies, which meant that they were treated worse than animals.

According to the ideology of the new masters, it was an unforgivable weakness for a true Communist to display human feelings such as compassion or mercy toward class enemies. A true Communist would demand that they fulfill their production obligations to the socialist society and would punish unmercifully any who did not fulfill their quotas.[3]

To anyone with some knowledge of entrepreneurial ecology it seems obvious that this policy of terrorism toward the producers would inhibit their will to work. And no terror or threats of terror could halt the steady decline in production that occurred.

During the first few years after 1917 the production of industrial goods fell to a fraction of its earlier volume. Since it is possible to survive without industrial products, this setback could be endured. Far worse was the steep decline in deliveries of food to the cities. The government tried to support the townspeople by having armed patrols search the farms, confiscating everything edible they could find, including livestock, seed grain, and the peasant families' own food.

By gradually slaughtering and eating the stock of domestic animals and by increasing the proportion of grain and vegetables in the diet, it was possible to meet the basic needs of the population—but just barely —during the first three years. But in 1921 the oppression and exploitation of the peasants ripened into disaster in the form of a dreadful famine.

Relief expeditions on a massive scale were sent from other countries. The most important was organized by the League of Nations under the leadership of the Norwegian Polar explorer Fridtjof Nansen, who was awarded the Nobel Peace Prize in 1922. The lives of twelve to thirteen million people were saved, but many millions more, most of them peasants, could not be prevented from starving to death.

The Lenin regime blamed the famine on poor harvests in the Ukraine and other Russian granaries that—according to the regime—were caused by droughts and bad weather. Lenin gave the tone, and his successors have consistently blamed crop failures on weather. The myth that Lenin created was believed, and the 1921 famine was interpreted as a natural catastrophe. Even today this myth is perpetuated in encyclopedias and history books.

Stalin's Legacy

If Stalin had wanted to read out the names of all those he had murdered, the task would have consumed all of his time.

Ilya Ehrenburg, Russian author, 1965

In the long run the Communists in power could not tolerate private capitalistic agriculture, and in 1928 Stalin felt sufficiently comfortable in the saddle to initiate a massive offensive to socialize the private peasants. The attack on private farms, which had increased in number to twenty-five million after 1917 as a consequence of the confiscation and division of the large estates, was motivated by more than ideology.

There was also an economy of scale: twenty-five million "ineffective" small family farms were to be replaced by larger, more effective units.

And there was an administrative motive: centrally managing and controlling a limited number of large enterprises is much easier than managing and controlling twenty-five million small farms.

The collectivization of Russian agriculture was carried out with ruthless brutality and terrorism. Lenin's oppression and exploitation of the peasants had brought about a catastrophic famine in the early 1920s. It should not have been difficult to foresee that Stalin's new wave of terrorism would pave the way for new disaster.

The result was a crop reduction with fatal consequences. According to the best available estimates—no official reports were ever published —between 1929 and 1933 five million people died of starvation and as many were liquidated by the regime, all together more than the total number of deaths in World War I.

At first glance it would appear that Stalin had learned nothing from Lenin's mistakes, specifically those that had caused the famine of the early 1920s. Stalin was, however, not so unintelligent. From all evidence, he seems to have been well aware of the costs and the consequences of his offensive against the peasants, the private "capitalistic" entrepreneurs of Russian agriculture. But to a fanatic like Stalin, no sacrifices in the forging of a socialist society could be too great.

And so a socialist agriculture, with large collective farms and state farms, was erected on the ruins of private agriculture. After a few years of intense suffering, socialist production increased, and from the mid-1930s it was able to meet the subsistence needs of the population.

Through economies of scale, new techniques, and modern machinery, the road to success in agricultural production appeared to lie open. Official reports also, in fact, boasted about socialist triumphs in food production.

Eventually, however, it was proven that the production of imposing statistical reports is easier than the production of imposing and sufficient quantities of food. No dictator can change the relentless decree of natural law—only food can cure starvation.

The spotlight first exposed the reality behind the official facade in 1953, after Stalin's death, when his successor, Nikita Khrushchev, revealed that Russia at that time had fewer livestock than it had had in 1913, in a society that had sixty million more people to feed than it had had before World War I.

Russian Agriculture after Stalin

We feared that the final victory of Socialism should be hampered and hindered if the truth about Stalin's paradise were revealed to the public.

Halldór Laxness, Icelandic author and Nobel Laureate, 1965

When, in 1954, Khrushchev revealed the truth about Russian agriculture, and blamed it on his predecessor, Stalin, he was fully optimistic that he could cure its ills. Despite some initial successes, however, he could not prevent the crop disaster of 1963, a failure that necessitated massive imports of grain from the West. The failure was a personal defeat for Khrushchev and strongly contributed to his fall in 1964.

For the next few years both the Russians and the rest of the world believed that the troubles were temporary and that with a new and better policy the situation would improve. And a new agricultural policy, along with more chemical fertilizers, more machines, and higher wages for the underpaid agricultural workers, was in fact promised by Khrushchev's successor, Leonid Brezhnev.

New agricultural policies and new investments had been promised so many times in the past, however, that few people believed in them. This time, too, the doubts proved well founded. The setback in 1963 was followed by new crop failures in 1965, 1972, 1975, 1979, 1980, 1981, 1982, and 1983, and steady increases in the volume of imports became necessary.

A study of crop figures for the fourteen years from 1970 to 1983, shown in the following table, reveals not merely a stagnation of production but a decline. The disastrous harvest of 165 million tons in 1981 occurred simultaneously with a record harvest of 331 million tons in the United States. For the first time in history, American output was twice that of Russia.

A closer study of the official Russian crop figures reveals remarkable things. The harvest volumes were so large in relation to the size of the population that—if the figures were correct—no import should have been necessary. According to published figures, the available quantities of grain per capita in the Soviet Union, including net imports, were 40 to 50 percent higher than the corresponding quantities per capita in the countries of the European Economic Community or in Sweden.

TABLE 1

GRAIN SUPPLY OF THE SOVIET UNION
(IN MILLIONS OF TONS)

Years	Amount Harvested	Goal	Amount Imported
1970	187 (record)	185	10
1971	181	190	8
1972	150	200	21
1973	220 (record)	205	22
1974	196	205	17
1975	140	215	30
1976	223 (record)	220	20
1977	194	225	12
1978	237 (record)	230	18
1979	179	230	32
1980	181	235	33
1981	(165)	238	37
1982	(170)	238	42
1983	190	238	(29)

Sources: Crop and target figures are regularly published in the official Russian Statistics, primarily in *Narkhoz, Narodnoe Khozyaistvo, SSSR* (Statistical Yearbook) Moscow. The import volumes have been obtained as a sum of export figures from the exporting countries. In contrast to previous years, no crop figures for 1981 and 1982 were published; the figures here are according to international expert estimates. Cf. Stefan Hedlund, *Crisis in Soviet Agriculture* (Sweden: University of Lund, 1983) and statistics continuously published by the U.S. Department of Agriculture. The figures in parentheses were not confirmed; the figure for 1983 was revealed by Konstantin Chernenko in his speech on March 2, 1984.

The differences can be explained in part. Because of the low output per hectare—only one-third that of the United States—the Russian farms have had to use some 16 percent of their harvest for seed, while only 2 percent is needed in the U.S.[4] But neither this nor the exceptionally large losses caused by careless handling or insufficient facilities for transportation and storage can explain the relatively high Russian crop figures. Other explanations are needed.

In order to avoid criticism—to say nothing of reprisal or punishment—Russian farm managers are constantly tempted to report greater volumes than are actually harvested. With factors such as this, the statistical accuracy of Russian harvest reports is highly suspect.

Despite promises of new investments and better policies, the trend toward imports has been rising steadily. In 1975, when the import volume reached 30 million tons, the capacity of the Russian ports—those of Riga and Odessa for example—was exceeded, and there were long lines and long waiting times for the ships. Since then the ports have been expanded and by 1982 were able to handle 42 million tons.

To be sure, grain is not the only foodstuff imported. Three million tons of sugar have been imported from Cuba regularly, and when the Russian sugar beet crop failed in 1980, Cuban sugar had to be supplemented with imports from other countries. Substantial quantities of meats are also imported, and in 1980 the Soviet Union was Argentina's largest customer for beef.

The ruling groups in all socialist countries base their power on the support of the industrial workers and the city dwellers, and they try to pay for this political support with a number of privileges, above all with cheap food. Low, controlled prices paid to the peasant producers are not sufficient. Consumer prices are generally reduced further with the help of state subsidies on basic foods, subsidies which in the early 1980s have amounted to approximately $20 billion a year in the Soviet Union.

To remain in favor, political leaders have usually preferred to increase subsidies rather than raise consumer prices and keep pace with inflation. In spite of doubled wages and salaries, therefore, the price of bread has remained at the same level for almost thirty years; a loaf of dark bread costs about fifteen cents and a loaf of white bread about twenty-five cents. These prices are so low that they encourage extravagance and waste; bread not consumed the day it is purchased is often thrown away.

This artificial pricing policy has meant that the price per kilogram of bread often is, in fact, lower than the price per kilogram of grain. Since peasants often find it difficult to obtain fodder for their private livestock, and since bread is sold freely, bread is often used as fodder in spite of threats of severe punishment.

Prices of beef and pork have also been kept artificially low, thereby stimulating consumption. According to United Nations statistics, Soviet annual consumption per capita in 1980 was 50 kilos. The corresponding figure in Sweden was 54 kilos and in the United States 79 kilos.[5]

Since 1980 the food supply situation in the Soviet Union has seriously deteriorated. In May 1981 an "experiment" in rationing meat and butter —the first rationing of such foods since World War II—was initiated in Irkutsk in Siberia. The rations were 1 kilo of meat and 300 grams of butter per person a month, quantities far below the average figures given in the official statistics. In 1982 and 1983 the "experiment" was extended to several other cities, and according to reports, not even these small rations could be delivered. For long periods the stores had no meat at all to sell.

If the politically manipulated food prices in the Soviet Union are not raised in the near future to a level at which supply and demand are in balance—and the evidence indicates that substantial price rises would be necessary if this goal were to be reached—it cannot be long before the rationing "experiment" will have to be applied to the whole country.

After a series of crop failures in 1981 and 1982, grain production statistics were no longer available. And after a serious increase of infant mortality after 1970, no more statistics concerning those realities were published either. But of course a gradually reduced food supply must have its consequences, and, according to official statistics *(Narodnoe Khozyaistvo)*, between 1965 and 1980 the mean expectation of life for Russian men has been reduced by four years.

The Soviet Union, the United States, and Sweden—A Comparison

> A small proprietor who knows every part of his little territory, who views it all with the affection which property, especially small property, naturally inspires, and who upon that account takes pleasure not only in cultivating but in adorning it, is generally of all improvers the most industrious, the most intelligent, and the most successful.
>
> *Adam Smith,* 1776

Agriculture is one of the few industries in which clear comparisons of productivity between different countries can be made. The percentage of the total labor force allocated to agriculture by each country is a good indicator.

In both the United States and Sweden, agricultural labor ranges from 3 to 4 percent of the total population, while in the Soviet Union it is 23 percent. It must further be noted that in the United States and Sweden the farmers produce substantial surpluses for export, while in the Soviet Union approximately one-third of the food supply must either be imported or produced on private plots which are not included in the Soviet agricultural statistics. As is shown in the following table, there are great differences in the agriculture of the three countries.

TABLE 2

The Structure of Agriculture in the United States, Sweden, and the Soviet Union, 1980

Country	Number of Farms Having Two or More Hectares in Cropland	Average Cropland per Farm (in Hectares)	Share of the Labor Force in Agriculture (%)
United States	2,400,000	70	3–4
Sweden	115,000	25	3–4
Soviet Union	145,000	1,500	23

Sources: USA: *Statistical Yearbook.* Sweden: *Jordbruksstatistisk årsbok.* Soviet Union: *Narkhoz, Narodnoe Khozyaistvo.*

In 1980 the large-scale agriculture in the Soviet Union consisted of only 47,000 enterprise units: 21,000 state farms with an average area of 19,000 hectares, of which 6,500 were under cultivation, and 26,000 collective farms with an average area of 6,400 hectares, of which 3,400 were under cultivation.

In addition, there were some 100,000 minor farms with an average area of 60 hectares, farms operated by corporations outside the agricultural sector in order to ensure a supply of food for their staff restaurants. The uncertainty of deliveries from socialist farms have forced the corporations to operate farms of their own.

With relatively few exceptions, agriculture in both the United States and Sweden is organized as family farms, the majority of which are owned entirely or in part by the farmers themselves. They are small enterprises, as a rule, operated by the members of the owner's family. Most are so small that they can be operated on a part-time basis by a family of whom one or several members are wage-earners employed away from the farm.

In both the United States and Sweden, most entrepreneurs are still private entrepreneurs. But outside agriculture they are so hampered and burdened by government regulations that they no longer can be labeled free entrepreneurs.

The government regulations within agriculture—unlike the regulations outside agriculture—are on the whole designed to support and protect the entrepreneurs, the farmers. While price controls outside agriculture force prices below the market level, controls within agriculture force prices above this level.

The farmers in these two countries can still be classified as free entrepreneurs, enjoying the privilege of operating according to their own preferences in an environment that gives them strong incentives to invest all their strength and creativity in their work and to do so without thought of regulated working hours or holidays.

Throughout the world it has been demonstrated that the small family farm, once so despised by the founders of socialism, is decidedly more efficient than the gigantic agricultural enterprises of socialist countries, as long as the farmer is allowed to work as a free entrepreneur.

From the beginning, agriculture in the Soviet Union has been treated as a stepchild, deprived of investments and resources. Poor agricultural production has been the consequence. During the Khrushchev era, however, from 1953 to 1964, and especially during the Brezhnev era from 1964 to 1983, the deprivations were replaced by a decidedly generous investment policy. The quantities of chemical fertilizers delivered to the farms increased steadily, and in 1981 26 million tons were used in the Soviet Union. Only 21 million tons were used in the United States.[6]

Soviet governments since Khrushchev have tried to cure the chronic ills of socialist agriculture with larger investments—more fertilizers, more machines, and so on—but despite these efforts, agriculture has steadily deteriorated. During recent years more than 25 percent of total Soviet investment has been in agriculture, a share unsurpassed among industrial countries.

The ills of socialist agriculture seem to be immune to materialistic remedies applied so far. The only logical conclusion is that the roots of the trouble must lie deeper, within the socialist system itself. The same conclusion is drawn by Lester R. Brown in an informative booklet in which he says:

> Soviet leaders may not yet have studied agricultural modernization elsewhere enough to see the inherent conflict between a centrally-planned agriculture and a highly productive agriculture. So far they have only attempted to improve the existing system, rather than turn away from centralized planning and control. But the problem is not that Soviet planners are unintelligent or that the Soviet farm labor force is lazy and inept. It is the faulty design of the system itself. It does not work effectively and cannot be expected to. Fixing the ills of Soviet agriculture without reforming the system will be like treating the symptoms of an illness rather than the cause. In

agriculture, as in medicine, the risk in such an approach is that the patient's condition may worsen.[7]

The large socialist agricultural enterprises in the Soviet Union manage to produce only enough food to supply two-thirds of the nation's domestic needs. The remainder is covered by production on 35 million private plots and by imports. In order to achieve full coverage of the need for food in the Soviet Union, it would be necessary to allocate at least 35 percent of the Russian labor force to socialist agriculture rather than the 23 percent so employed now. Some allowance for decreasing yields must be included in such a calculation.

In both the U.S. and Sweden, more than enough food to satisfy domestic needs is produced by 3.5 percent of the labor force. It would seem that private agriculture in these countries is approximately ten times as efficient as socialist agriculture in the Soviet Union.

Private Peasants in the Soviet Union

Owning a piece of land gives the peasant an interest and a willingness to work; it is this that will encourage increased prosperity.

Gunnar Myrdal, 1964

During the trying years of collectivization in the early 1930s, Stalin was forced to permit the peasants to cultivate their own plots to meet the needs of their families and—to relieve the starving city dwellers—to permit them to sell their surpluses at free prices on free markets, the kolkhoz markets in nearby towns and cities. Today there are thirty such markets in Moscow and approximately 8,000 in the entire country.

Since private wholesalers, according to socialist ideology, are profiteers, kolkhoz markets are permitted only for peasants who personally transport their products to the markets and personally sell them there. Such a distribution system is of course highly impractical and inefficient, and in recent years minor rationalizations have been permitted.

The permanent crisis of socialist agriculture and the constant scarcity of food explains why these peasants have been able to sell their surpluses from the plots at very good prices. It also explains why the members of their families, primarily the housewives, have gladly devoted their spare hours to cultivation of the plots.

According to recent reports, however, young people are becoming more and more reluctant to use their leisure time in this way; they are tired of milking the cow, feeding the pigs and poultry, and cleaning out the stables. The, so far, highly necessary stream of food from the private plots to the cities has therefore tended to shrink during recent years and will probably shrink further in the future.

To be sure, private agriculture was a foreign element in socialist society, and according to the political leaders it was to be eliminated as soon as the socialist farms had left their infant maladies behind them and were able to satisfy the needs of the country themselves.

After the gigantic cultivation campaign in Kazakhstan (1953-60) and after a few good harvests there, Khrushchev felt so confident that in his ideological arrogance he started a campaign against the private plots. But a disastrous crop in 1963 followed.

Khrushchev's successors learned their lessons, and proclaimed that the food produced on private plots was virtually indispensable. They had to conclude that the socialist farms probably never would be able to produce enough food for the country themselves, and reacted by granting the private peasants somewhat better terms than they had enjoyed earlier.

Today there are some 35 million plots—private mini-farms—in the Soviet Union, with a maximum area of 0.25 hectares each; the average size is close to 0.2 hectares. Some basic information about the mini-farms and their production is presented here.

TABLE 3

PRIVATE AGRICULTURE IN THE SOVIET UNION, 1977

Number of plots: 35,000,000
Total area in hectares: 8,000,000
Percentage of total cropland area: 3
Percentage of total agricultural output: 27;
    of beef and pork, 30; of milk, 30; of eggs, 38;
    of vegetables, 32; of potatoes, 56

Sources: *Literaturnaya Gazeta* 1977, as quoted in *Dagens Nyheter,* May 22, 1977, and Stefan Hedlund, *Crisis in Soviet Agriculture* (University of Lund, Economic Studies 28, 1983), pp. 117 ff.

In the centrally planned, controlled, and regulated socialist Soviet economy there is only one legal island of freedom, the mini-farms. The cultivators of these plots plan and organize their work entirely as they wish and are in the true meaning of the term free entrepreneurs. They sell their surpluses at free prices in free markets, and they pay neither sales taxes nor income taxes. In a miraculous way the mini-farms function as free economic zones within a socialist environment.[8]

An Incentive-Killing System

The politicians, by following their usual course, exploit the food producers in order to secure the political support of the urban masses. By and large, farmers do not trust politicians. They have good reason. Too often they have either been ignored or exploited by them. It is painfully apparent that almost all government interventions in the food supply system result in a reduction of food supply. The food problem is primarily a political problem.

Merrit L. Kastens, American agricultural expert, 1981

Socialist Soviet agriculture is, as already noted, decidedly inefficient. The fact that the great majority of American farmers own their farms, wholly or in part, has often—from romantic notions about freeholding farmers—been offered as the key to their efficiency; nonownership therefore is assumed to be the reason for inefficiency in socialist agriculture. Despite the undeniably stimulating effect of ownership, however, it does not sufficiently explain the enormous difference between the efficiency of private agriculture and that of socialized agriculture. Comparative studies of owned and leased farms in the United States and Sweden have shown that the differences are not of great significance.

According to another explanation, socialist gigantomania should be a burden that lies heavy on Soviet agriculture, lessening its productivity. The average area of the 21,000 state farms is 19,000 hectares, an area so large that if it were a square each side would measure fourteen kilometers. The average area of the 26,000 collective farms is 6,400 hectares, an area that corresponds to an eight-kilometer square. Even if it is conceded that such units are far beyond optimal size, however—internal transport, for example, must be long and expensive—gigantomania alone can explain only part of the difference. In both the United States and Sweden, large farms and estates are usually as productive as smaller units.

The firm socialist belief in economies of scale has dictated structural changes in Soviet agriculture. While in 1940 there were 235,000 collective farms, by 1965 their number had been reduced to 37,000 collective farms, and by 1980 to 26,000. The hopes of the regime, however, rest on the true socialist enterprises, the gigantic state farms, the number of which increased from 12,000 in 1965 to 21,000 in 1980. As late as February 1976—after the severe crop failure of 1975—Brezhnev expressed his conviction that even larger enterprises would lead to greater efficiency in Soviet agriculture.

A third explanation is that central planning and control paralyze the initiative of local managers. In an article on the Soviet harvest catastrophe of 1975, Peter G. Lindberg discusses the "rigidly centralized system" as the cause of the failure:

> From the central organization a flood of papers comes with directives regulating the smallest details. Paper work will consume more time than the actual running of the farm. The press is, to be sure, well aware of this. According to a report in *Pravda* a manager at a kolkhoz during a six-month period received 800 directives from different authorities. In addition, there were discussions and investigations, often focused on efforts to find political scapegoats.[9]

In pointing to central control, the core of socialism, Mr. Lindberg points to the fundamental cause.

There are, of course, other contributing causes. The terror suffered by peasants under Lenin and Stalin survives as a vivid memory for descendants of the victims. The peasants, from the beginning of the socialist regime, have had good reason to consider themselves an ill-treated and exploited outgroup. Last of all to be granted state old-age pensions and minimum wages, they received the former only in 1965 and the latter in 1966. And as late as 1976, when the minimum pension for other citizens was 45 rubles a month, the peasants had to be content with 20 rubles. This kind of discrimination further lowers the working morale of the socialized peasants.

Soviet Peasants—Slave Labor

The problem is not how the Soviet Union will find a way out of totalitarianism, but how the West will be able to avoid the Soviet fate.

Alexander Solzhenitsyn, 1982

Significantly higher incomes, better housing, and better working conditions of people in nonagricultural fields have served as a strong incentive for the young in the Soviet countryside to migrate from the farms. But since food has been in chronically short supply, such migration has been forbidden. In 1932 Stalin introduced a system of domestic passports in order to stop the migration. No one was allowed to leave his place of residence for more than forty-eight hours without a written permit. The possession of a passport was a prerequisite for a permit, but the peasants were denied passports and thus deprived of any legal right to leave their home areas. Serfdom in Russia, which had been abolished in 1861 by Czar Alexander II, was thus, in effect, reintroduced in 1932.

Since Khrushchev's revelations concerning Stalin at the Twentieth Party Congress in 1956, the oppression of the peasants under Stalin has been well known. Less known is the fact that the serfdom of the peasants that he reintroduced was retained for decades by his successors. Not until the mid-1970s were domestic passports issued to the peasants, and even then not all at once, but gradually throughout the period 1976–1981.

Czar Alexander's reform liberated 23 million serfs from their bonds, while Brezhnev's reform granted greater freedom to 32 million Russians. The freedom of all Russians is still limited, however, by the system of domestic passports, which is still in effect. Yet the bonds have been loosened somewhat: In 1976 all Russians carrying valid passports were granted the right to leave their home areas for as long as six weeks without police permits.

Oppression and exploitation can only kill the incentive to produce. This is the root of the inefficiency that characterizes Soviet agriculture. The workers who handle heavy farm machinery—tractors, harvestors, and the like—are so careless with it that many of the machines are abused and unusable.

Adam Smith, in *The Wealth of Nations*, showed great insight into the inefficiency and lack of inventiveness in the oppressed:

> The experience of all ages and nations, I believe, demonstrates that the work done by slaves, though it appears to cost only their maintenance, is in the end the dearest of any. A person who can acquire no property, can have no other interest but to eat as much, and to labour as little as possible. Whatever work he does beyond what is sufficient to purchase his own maintenance can be squeezed out of him by violence only, and not by any interest of his own. . . .
>
> Slaves are very seldom inventive. All the most important improvements, either in machinery, or in the arrangement and distribution of work, which facilitate and abridge labour, have been the discoveries of freemen. Should a slave propose any improvement of this kind, his master would be very apt to consider the proposal as the suggestion of laziness, and of a desire to save his own labour at the master's expense. The poor slave, instead of reward, would probably meet with much abuse, perhaps with some punishment.[10]

The Slave Laborers' Secret Weapon

> If the workers and peasants do not wish to accept socialism, our reply will be: Why waste words when we can apply force?
>
> *V. I. Lenin,* 1918

When the founding fathers of the Soviet state set out in 1917 to build a socialist state, they started from an unlimited belief in the powers of force and terror. The state coercion apparatus was their primary instrument, and they assumed that the multitude of peasants could be frightened and forced to work as feudal serfs in the service of the socialist state, which is to say, in the service of the men in power. Experience soon proved, however, that their faith in the power of force was unjustified. The story of Soviet agricultural policy is not only the story of numerous assaults by the regime on the peasants but also the story of as many retreats.

The struggle between the peasant masses and the Red masters, which has been going on since 1917, has been neither organized nor heroic on the part of the peasants. They have not fought in underground resistance movements or in partisan groups, and, despite accusations that they have done so, they have seldom deliberately sabotaged production. But oppression and exploitation have killed their incentives to work.

On the one side of this struggle have stood the Red masters, armed with the state coercion apparatus, the power to set low prices on agricultural products, and the power to compel deliveries. And also armed with a frightening terror apparatus: well-equipped police forces and soldiers, prisons, slave camps, execution platoons.

On the other side have stood the peasant masses, poor and unarmed, apparently helpless before the might of the masters. The unarmed peasants, however, hold a secret weapon. Only peasants can produce food, and, if sufficient food is not produced, if shortages and famines arise, the existence of the regime is at stake. While the existence of the peasants is not dependent on the regime, the existence of the regime is entirely dependent on the peasants.

The Soviet masters can oppress, exploit, mistreat, terrorize, and murder the peasants. But they can never do it without suffering severe consequences in the form of reduced production and an insufficient food supply.

Food Production and National Power

As long as capitalism and socialism exist side by side we cannot live in peace. In the end, one of them will conquer. A funeral hymn will be sung either over the Soviet Union or over world capitalism.

V. I. Lenin, 1918

As stressed earlier, one of the fundamental characteristics of Soviet agricultural policy is its incentive-killing effects on food production. Similar policies are followed in almost all socialist countries. As a consequence, more and more countries that once were not only self-supporting but were actually producing and exporting surpluses are now forced to rely on imports. Russia, before the Revolution the world's greatest exporter of grain, has now become the world's greatest grain importer —42 million tons in 1982. Japan, for decades the greatest importer of wheat, was surpassed by the Soviet Union in 1975. During the early 1980s the volume of the Soviet import became twice that of Japan.

The only positive element that can be discerned in this low production level in the socialist countries is the enormous unrealized production potential. If one day in the future an incentive-stimulating policy will be substituted for the present incentive-killing policy, enormous food-production powers will be released.

The present agricultural policy in the socialist countries has not only a supply aspect but also a power aspect. Every country that cannot satisfy its food needs with its own production resources becomes dependent on imports and thereby on the goodwill of other countries. And the greater the volume of imports needed, the greater the dependence will be. This kind of import dependency can be exploited politically by the exporters. It is by no means always sufficient for the importing countries to pay cash in hard currency for the food import; beyond that, they are often forced to adapt their domestic and foreign policies to the interests and evaluations of the exporter.

The problem of ensuring sufficient food for a country always has a military aspect. Reasons of defense have always been used to justify Swedish agricultural policy, with its favors and subsidies for farmers. No matter how expensive and strong the military forces of a country, if its own agricultural production is not sufficient to feed itself during a war, the country may be forced to capitulate to an enemy if prevented from importing food by means of a blockade.

The power aspect takes on a fateful quality when it is remembered that the market system has stimulated the development of a highly efficient food-production apparatus in the Western world, while the Eastern socialist system has had the opposite effect. As a consequence, one of the world's two superpowers, the United States, is the greatest exporter of food—in the early 1980s it exported 55 percent of all food sold on the world market—while the other, the Soviet Union, is the world's greatest importer of food.

In certain situations great food surpluses can be used as instruments of extortion. Food-supply superiority can be used in the same way as military superiority. The "wheat bomb" can be used for threats and blackmail in the same way as the atomic bomb.

When the Soviet Union on December 27, 1979, invaded Afghanistan, it took only until January 5, 1980, for President Carter to stop the greater part of the planned export of grain to the Soviet Union—17 million tons out of a total of 25 million tons. Only the 8 million that had been sold on federal long-term contracts were released.

This maneuver was only partly successful, for such countries as Argentina saw an opportunity to sell grain to the Soviet Union at prices twice as high as those they had accepted earlier. Anyhow the Soviet Union was able on this occasion to compensate for reduced American shipments by means of increased imports from other countries.

The vulnerability of the Soviet Union in war because of the large amount of food that it must import should not be overemphasized, however. In its ample production of animal food and its high consumption of beef and pork per capita, the Soviet Union has an important reserve. By shifting in their diet from animal foods, which are highly resource-consuming, to vegetables, which are lowly resource-consuming—as took place in many countries during World War II—the Russians would be able to satisfy their basic requirements for food.

The steadily increasing dependence of most socialist countries on imported food, however, puts them at other grave disadvantages. More and more of their export income is consumed as payment for imports of food, which means that less and less is left to pay for the import of necessary raw materials, machines, and industrial commodities, imports that could have accelerated economic growth.

Until now a great many socialists countries have been able, on the whole, to finance their growing imports of food with the help of credits from the West. By borrowing they have been able to live beyond their means for long periods. Sooner or later, however, their credit potential will have been consumed, and it will no longer be possible to postpone the real difficulties.

Chapter 3

Poland

> The Polish nation, not so much alive as surviving, persists in thinking, breathing, speaking, hoping, and suffering in a land most of all like a grave, railed in by a million bayonets.
>
> *Joseph Conrad,* 1911

The Writing on the Wall

> Most of those who advocate socialism do so in the genuine belief that they will thereby assist the poor and most deserving elements of our population.
>
> *F. A. Hayek,* 1977

Since August 1980, when the supply problems and the political conflicts in Poland had developed into a crisis, there has been a deluge of information about the situation. This information, however, resembles nothing so much as a heap of pieces of a puzzle. Not until the pieces have been put in order can patterns and causal relations be seen.

The shortage of goods and a shortage of food so severe that it threatened to develop into a famine were interpreted by most people as the result of some kind of natural disaster, primarily bad weather. Those in power in Poland, who for at least six years have blamed the increasing shortages and the ever longer lines outside the stores on bad weather, accepted this primitive interpretation gratefully.

The geographic and climatic conditions for agriculture in Poland are excellent, however, and before the Communists took over and converted a plus into a minus, Poland was one of Europe's granaries, with large export surpluses. When agricultural production in such a country continuously decreases, some questions must be asked: What policies against the producers—in this case the peasants—have been pursued by those who hold power? Have these policies meant oppression and exploitation of the producers? Have they damaged the entrepreneurial environment, including production incentives?

Treatment of the Private Peasants

There is something in the collectivist system that does not agree with our nature, that does not mobilize our best qualities.

Uno Lamm, Swedish technological innovator, 1979

An automobile with the best of motors cannot function without fuel. Human beings without incentives will not work. The stronger the incentives, the better the results.

Experience in capitalist countries has proved that free farmers, working in a favorable entrepreneurial environment with real rewards for their production, are willing to invest themselves in long working days, usually with neither free weekends nor vacations. In Poland, however, agriculture is an extraordinarily inefficient industry. One-third of the population is employed in agriculture, but despite this enormous input of manpower, production cannot meet the domestic need for food. In the United States and Sweden, only a tenth of that share of the labor force is engaged in agriculture but is able to produce large surpluses for export.

Following World War II the Communist regime in Poland planned to transform Polish agriculture from a system encompassing millions of small private farms into one of gigantic state or collective farms, thereby following the Soviet pattern of large "efficient" enterprises. For various reasons this plan was abandoned, and when the Communist leader Wladyslaw Gomulka signaled retreat in the mid-1950s, 80 percent of the cropland remained in private hands. Since then the socialized sector has slowly but steadily been extended, and as this is being written, in 1983, the private peasants still cultivate roughly 70 percent of the cropland.

Long experience in the West has proved that an agricultural sector with private farmers can function in a highly efficient way; why does an agriculture in which most farms are privately held function so poorly in Poland?

As in the Soviet Union, the Polish political leaders receive their support from the industrial and urban population and must pay for that support with privileges, among them cheap food, a privilege provided at the expense of the peasants. In a socialist country with private agriculture, the groups in power exploit the peasants through price control. Prices for the foodstuffs produced by the peasants are set far below the prices that the consumers would have been willing to pay in free markets. The peasants have good reason to feel robbed.

Also, even if the legal right to own land has been formally retained for private peasants in Poland, land ownership has in reality been undermined by having been changed into a right to use the land during the active time of the "owner." This restricted ownership produces only weak incentives for championing, developing, and improving the farms.

Against this background it is easy to explain the backwardness of Polish agriculture. The consequences were such that the regime in January 1983 had to promise to restore ownership to the peasants. With price control as an instrument, those in power have deprived the peasants of the capital that would have enabled them to invest in their farms —to buy machinery, chemical fertilizers, good seed, good livestock, and so on. When a farmer in the West invests in improvements to his farm, he feels confident that he will be remunerated in a future sale. This strong incentive to make improvements is lacking in Polish agriculture, where other people besides the peasants harvest the rewards.

Political Prices Instead of Free-Market Prices

> Sooner or later democracy in Poland is bound to win over its enemies.
>
> *Czeslaw Milosz,* 1981

In a socialist country such as Poland, the industrial and urban population—the groups supporting the regime—expect rewards and privileges; they expect some progress toward prosperity. The demand for higher standards becomes a demand for higher wages and stable prices.

The Polish governments have not been able to prevent inflation, including increases in wages and income. Food prices, however, have been kept stable by means of price controls. As inflation has forced the authorities to raise the peasants' delivery prices, they have been able to maintain stable consumer prices only with the help of state subsidies. Every year the gap between producer prices and consumer prices has widened, a development that has demanded ever-increasing subsidies. This has meant that the government, confronted with ever-increasing demands for state money, has had to allocate growing shares of resources—funds sorely needed for other purposes—for food subsidies.

Those in power have often realized that this trend must be stopped. In December 1970 Gomulka, Communist Party Chairman between 1956 and 1970, decreed that food prices be increased by 50 to 100 percent. Price increases of this magnitude were, of course, perceived by consumers as something of a catastrophe.

The Poles exploded. They protested, demonstrated, and went on strike. Workers at the large shipyards on the Baltic took the lead, and rage reached such proportions that a revolutionary fervor developed—it was a situation so critical that only a major political "sacrifice" could calm it. Gomulka was forced to resign; he was succeeded in January 1971 by Edward Gierek, and all price-raising plans were abandoned.

Gierek rapidly restored order with generous promises of cheap food, major investments, and rising prosperity. With massive new loans from the West, those promises were actually fulfilled for some years.

By 1975 the cost of food subsidies had, however, risen to a level where they consumed 25 percent of the national budget—an unreasonable amount for a poor country. Radical price increases could no longer be postponed. Strangely, the entire drama of 1970 was repeated. On Midsummer Day, June 24 of 1975, Prime Minister Piotr Jaroszewicz announced that prices would be increased by 60 to 100 percent, and, exactly as in 1970, strikes and demonstrations, with violent riots, exploded throughout the country. The government was forced to retreat again and promise that prices would remain unchanged. Gierek, in an acrobatic effort, managed to stay in the saddle. Incredibly, Gierek succeeded once more in mobilizing gigantic credits in the West, and postponing the inevitable problem of mounting deficits.

But the credit-road dalliance is always bound to end, and the potential for more credits abroad will be exhausted eventually. In Poland this point was reached in 1980, when a rise in prices became unavoidable. For a third time the drama was reenacted. To calm the desperate masses, another great political "sacrifice" was needed, and this time Party Chairman Gierek was forced to resign. His successor, Stanislaw Kania, never did succeed in gaining control, and the reigns of power came into the hands of the military. In October 1981 Kania, too, resigned; he was succeeded by General Wojciech Jaruzelski.

A power struggle developed between Jaruzelski's military junta and the independent trade union Solidarity, which had nearly 10 million members, and had been declared legal by the Supreme Court in November 1980. In the face of a volcanic civil uprising, a state of emergency imposing martial law and a curfew was proclaimed on December 13, 1981. Thousands of Solidarity leaders were arrested and placed in prisons and concentration camps. Many lives were lost in confrontations between workers and the military. In October 1982 the military government declared Solidarity illegal.

By February 1982 the government felt strong enough to proclaim and realize price increases that had been postponed for more than a decade. According to official reports, the cost of living increased more than 100 percent; food prices alone increased 150 percent. It was subsequently stated that the standard of living had decreased 25 percent during the preceding year.

With martial law in effect, the Poles had no choice but to accept the price increases and tighten their belts. There was no longer a big demand for cheap food; long lines outside the food stores grew shorter and even disappeared.

Politicians throughout the world generally interpret military takeovers such as that in Poland as undemocratic and unjustified, and in some cases such an interpretation is correct. In Poland it is obvious that those in power had for decades pursued a policy based on delusions. Necessary decisions and measures that were unpopular had been continually postponed. This policy only paved the way to famine and national disaster. Not until the situation had become critical did the military consider it its duty to act and realize those necessary economic reforms that for so many years had been postponed by weak "populist" governments.

When martial law, proclaimed on December 13, 1981, was officially abolished on July 22, 1983, that measure was only symbolic. The military junta still held Poland and its tenuous economy in an iron grip.

A Socialist Prescription against Food Shortages

The welfare state entirely neglects that the market is a process of information and mobilization of knowledge, a neglect with dramatic consequences. Poland is the best proof. For the first time we see an industrialized nation threatened by starvation.

Henri Lepage, French economist, 1983

In 1980 when large Polish imports of grain for fodder had to cease because credit was no longer available, meat production declined rapidly. Annual consumption of meat and pork still amounted to 150 pounds per person in 1979. The corresponding figure in August 1980, after rationing had been introduced, was 95 pounds; by December of that year it had fallen to 79, and one year later in January 1982 it was 66 pounds. Lines outside the stores indicated that the supply was insufficient even for these reduced rations.

More and more of the blame for the food shortage was placed on the peasants, who were accused of "speculative stockpiling" in expectation that shortages would force the government to raise prices. According to the authorities, less than half the quantities of food planned and "promised" by the peasants had been delivered.

As is common in socialist states, producer prices for food were pegged at an unreasonably low level. Neither production nor deliveries to the state purchasers were likely to be stimulated by such low prices.

If the authorities had listened to the market signals and obeyed them, they would have raised prices. But because price rises are unpopular, they followed the traditional socialist pattern and tried to force the peasants to produce and deliver, although compulsory deliveries had been formally abolished in Poland in 1972.

A leading Polish Communist, Professor J. B. Mazurkiewicz, head of the party's University for Social Sciences, wrote in the party newspaper that compulsory deliveries "are probably the only way to solve the food problem." He rationalized his conclusion by saying: "We have gradually reintroduced the socialist principle of compulsory work in the cities and factories. Why should we not apply the same principle to the peasants?"[11]

Declarations of this type bode ill for Poland and raise questions whether these Communists, blinded by dogma, are able to learn from experience. The lesson has not been learned although it is simple enough: To oppress and exploit the peasant is to reduce food production, make supply scarce, and pave the way to destitution.

In a Fool's Paradise of Borrowing

The Marxists have to realize that what has happened in the Soviet Union, in China, Cuba, Vietnam, and most recently in Poland and Yugoslavia is not a result of temporary mistakes or faults of single leaders but an inevitable consequence of the socialist system.

Andres Küng, Swedish economist, 1982

Poland's debt to the West increased from $4 billion in 1974 to $26 billion in 1983. With the help of massive loans, Gierek was able for many years to create an artificial economic boom by means of large investments and rapidly increasing production and consumption. During these years he was of course a popular leader.

The Poles lived, however, in a fool's paradise, and troubles emerged by the late 1970s. Not only were all domestic capital resources spent, but also the country's potential credit abroad was exhausted. In March 1981 Poland was forced to suspend payment of debt service, and after negotiations with the lenders an agreement was signed by which all amortization payments were to be postponed, although interest payments would be made.

But not even these reduced obligations could be met, and in April 1982 a new agreement was signed, granting postponement of the major part of the debt service for a period of up to seven years. Finally, in June 1982 the Polish government informed five hundred Western banks that without new credits the interest falling due in 1982—$2 billion—could not be paid; and after new negotiations in August 1983, practically all payments falling due in 1983 were postponed.

In reality, Poland today is bankrupt. The reason a declaration of default has not been issued is that the lenders are simply unwilling to take measures that would force them to write off claims and report losses so large that the stability of the banking community would be undermined.

In 1983 Poland's debt to fifteen Western countries and five hundred Western banks totaled $26 billion. Total debt obligations that fell due in 1982 amounted to roughly $10 billion, while the Polish export to the West earned only $5 billion. This means that the debt service that Poland was obliged to pay amounted to 200 percent of its export income.

Debt service equal to 20 percent of export income is usually considered the maximum that a country can manage to pay without assistance from new borrowing. That limit was exceeded by Poland as early as 1974. Obligations such as those Poland has in the 1980s can be paid only as long as gigantic new credits can be obtained. It is clear that a nation pursuing this kind of credit policy is living far beyond its means, consuming and investing much more than it is able to produce with its own resources.

In Poland, the artificial credit boom meant that all of Polish industry had adapted itself to a continuous supply of imported inputs and had become dependent on it. When credits from abroad ceased in 1981, Polish imports had to be reduced drastically, and severe withdrawal pains rocked Polish industry.

The machines in the factories were largely imported from the West and could function only as long as spare parts could be imported for their maintenance and repair. Production, moreover, was to a large extent based on imported raw materials and semimanufactures from the

TABLE 4

GROWTH OF FOREIGN DEBT POLAND, 1973–1980

Item	1973	1974	1975	1976	1977	1978	1979	1980
Total debt (in billions of dollars)	3	5	8	11	14	17	23	27
Debt-service obligation (in billions of dollars)	0.5	1.0	1.5	2.1	3.1	4.5	6.3	8.0
Debt-service obligation (as a percentage of GNP)	15	20	25	35	45	60	75	80

Source: From a report on the economic situation published in July 1981 by the Ministry of Finance, Warsaw. The figures include obligations to both the West and the East.

West. When, in 1980, these imports were radically reduced and in 1981 came to a stop in many fields, the consequences were catastrophic. Total production (GNP) decreased 2 percent in 1979, 4 percent in 1980, 13 percent in 1981, and 8 percent in 1982—a total production decrease during these four years of 25 percent.

Not only was a state of emergency and martial law proclaimed in December 1981, work was decreed compulsory and a general ban on strikes was issued. This duty to work—a euphemism for forced labor —applied to all men between the ages of eighteen and forty-five. Strict military discipline prevailed in all work places. A socialist system functions best with the help of force and terror; during the more lenient regimes of Gierek and Kania, the result had been chaos. Only by martial law could socialist order be restored.

The Concept of "Democratic" Socialism

"Liberal socialism" as the majority of people in the Western world understand it, is purely theoretical, while practical socialism is totalitarian everywhere.

F. A. Hayek, 1945

Political developments in Poland from the end of World War II to December 1981 produced a kind of populist "democratic" socialism. While in socialist states such as the Soviet Union, in which there is military and police dictatorship, the people must passively accept the decrees of the regime, the Polish people had opportunities to express feelings of dissatisfaction and protest and expressed them so energetically that time after time the government was forced to retreat from earlier positions and proclamations.

Price increases in free markets take place from day to day in small steps accepted by consumers, while as a rule the politically controlled prices in socialist economies are kept constant for long periods, often for decades. As it becomes necessary to raise wages and producer prices, unbearable economic tensions are eventually created, and sooner or later consumer prices must also be raised. Since a need for price increase can accumulate for many years in a socialist economy, prices are often raised by 50 to 100 percent in a single stroke. Consumers, of course, find such price explosions unbearable; in Poland, their reaction was so potentially "revolutionary" that successive governments were forced to retreat.

"Democratic" socialism is programmed with a developmental pattern, a road followed to the bitter end in Poland. It makes for an extremely unstable political system, doomed to rapid collapse and military takeover. The developments in Poland—as well as in Czechoslovakia in 1968—have been entirely logical.

A market system is fundamentally a nonviolent system; prices are determined by the relation between supply and demand, and buyers and sellers negotiate transactions freely. But a socialist system is built entirely on coercion. In a socialist state people are prohibited from acting freely as producers and consumers, as buyers and sellers, prohibited from negotiating and reaching agreements on employment, wages, production, prices, and quantities. All production and sales must take place under conditions determined by the government, conditions that could not be imposed for a single day without threat of brutal reprisal against disobedient citizens. Capital punishment is still a normal Soviet penalty for economic crimes—"crimes against the state." In April 1982, for instance, a former Soviet minister of fishing was summarily executed for corruption.

Never has socialism in the Soviet Union functioned better than under Stalin's reign of terror. The discipline in industry and society was total. Production increased steadily, and the country developed a military striking power surprising to all—not least to Hitler.

Despite the degrees of discipline that can be imposed, however, it is the basic concepts in socialist economies that are flawed and remain unaddressed. The fact is that sooner or later the cheap-food policy, a policy unanimously and energetically demanded and supported by the nonagrarian population, can only lead to dangerous reductions in food production and supply. But because the pressure for cheap food is strong, particularly in a system that allows for some popular expression, the self-defeating price policy is often pursued until the bitter end. No one ever tells the public the truth about the policy—so the nation pursues it in good conscience.

When at the end of 1981 severe food shortages in Poland arose, the independent trade unions in the Solidarity organization—as representatives of the consumers—threatened to call a general strike to emphasize their demands for cheap and sufficient food. The threat alone demonstrated the public's ignorance and inability to understand the real causes of the scarcities and of their own hunger. A general strike would, in fact, have worsened, not improved, the supply situation. Before the strike was called, however, the military took control. After February 1982, when the military government raised both consumer prices and producer prices drastically, the supply situation began to improve. But the problems continue, and the merry-go-round does not stop. Facing new price increases in 1984—urgently needed in order to prevent even worse shortages—the two champions of the people, the Church and Solidarity, made their grievances known. Despite the protests, the price increases were effectuated on January 31, 1984.

Political Prices and Waste

> Marxist revolutions lead to results completely differing from the noble purposes of the revolutionary pioneers.
>
> *Arthur Koestler,* 1945

In free markets, prices will stay at levels at which quantities supplied and demanded are approximately equal; in these balanced markets, neither shortages nor surpluses occur. In Poland, the politically determined food prices were regularly set below the balance level. As a consequence, demand exceeded supply, with shortages as a result. When food is in short supply and rationing has not been introduced, people will stand in line to buy what is available; in recent years, lines outside the stores have been a "normal" feature of Polish street life. As a rule, the public fails to understand that politically determined low prices inevitably create shortages.

While high prices stimulate thrift, low prices stimulate extravagance. In the spring of 1981 in Poland, an 800-gram loaf of dark rye bread still sold for four zloty—approximately ten cents—which meant that everyone thought he could afford to eat newly baked bread. As in the Soviet Union, bread not eaten on the day purchased is often thrown away, and bread not sold on the day baked is used for fodder. And, because of large subsidies, the price of bread in Poland has as a rule been lower than the price of fodder grain. Under such circumstances, the peasants with private plots have been tempted to use bread for fodder in spite of legal prohibitions against it. A completely absurd situation arose in which livestock were fed bread while some consumers—those last in the lines —in front of empty shops had to do without.

In a similar way, the extraordinarily low prices of meat—in 1980 a pound of beef still cost roughly 68 cents—stimulated excessive consumption. During the past ten or fifteen years annual consumption of beef and pork per capita has been higher in Poland than in Sweden: Already in 1970 112 pounds per person were consumed in Poland compared to 110 in Sweden; by 1979 the amounts had increased to 150 pounds in Poland and 121 in Sweden.[12]

In only a few of the world's richest countries could people afford to consume as much meat as they did in Poland. And Poland is not a rich country. Only by means of politically manipulated prices and at the expense of other consumption, of reduced investments, or of heavy foreign borrowing could this luxury consumption be maintained.

In free markets, prices are normally proportional to production costs, while in socialist economies deviations can be wide. No matter how prices are manipulated, however, the real costs of production have to be paid in one way or another. When goods are sold to consumers in Poland for a fraction of their real production costs, other costs are usually paid by consumers in the form of lower standards elsewhere.

A substantial share of the real costs in Poland seems to have been paid by countries in the West in the form of loans made by commercial and central banks. Because of the bankruptcy of the Polish state, these loans will most likely never be repaid.

In 1981 nearly 50 percent of the Polish national budget went to food subsidies, giving strong incentive to luxury consumption and waste. For a poor country like Poland, such an allocation seems irrational. The resources so used were, in fact, deeply needed for investment in a primitive and backward industry. Poland is a socialist country with a so-called planned economy. Can an economy that espouses policies such as those described here really be called a planned one?

Distribution by Prices, Coupons, and Queues

In a country where writers are silenced and driven into exile, you will inevitably find housewives in lines outside the stores.

Michel Tournier, French author, 1982

To ensure adequate food supply in a country, the peasants must be granted adequate incentives to produce. But no amount of production will suffice in the absence of a rational distribution system.

In a country with free markets, distribution is achieved by the agency of free prices. Since every resource is limited, every distribution system must entail some kind of a rationing system to control consumption. In a market economy, the ceiling on purchases—and consumption—is set by limited incomes—"rationing through the purse." In socialist states with politically decided prices, this kind of distribution system is rejected. There, consumer prices are as a rule set below the balance level, a level at which shortages are inevitable.

Theoretically, distribution in such an economy could be performed by means of rationing coupons. All experience indicates, however, that consumers' dislike of small rations is as strong as their dislike of price increases and high prices. So pressures from consumers have usually caused those in power to retreat from their original small rations and grant rations the sum of which has exceeded supplies. If demand exceeds supply because rations are too large, some consumers will receive no rations. Which consumers these will be is likely to be determined by their positions in the lines outside the stores.

Until the drastic price increases of February 1982, the distribution of food in Poland had been largely determined in this way. Aside from the fact that standing in lines requires an enormous waste of personal time and working capacity, a waste particularly absurd in a poor country, this is a deeply unsocial form of distribution. Those who are strong, healthy, and able to rise early in the morning—or even before morning—will get the places at the head of the line and will have a chance to buy. And because of low prices, the purchasers who make it to the counter often buy more than they would otherwise.

A society that distributes in this way is, in reality, a class society, with one privileged class consuming more than it needs and an underprivileged class consuming little or nothing. Many parents of small children cannot stand in lines, others are prevented from doing so by their jobs, still others cannot do so because of ill health, handicaps, or old age.

But even for the healthy, standing in line for several hours is trying. Since it must be done in all kinds of weather, it can be a threat to the consumer's health. A distribution system that forces people to waste unreasonable amounts of time and strength, and even forces them to risk their health must be considered an unsocial and inhuman system.

Aid from Abroad

The Polish economic crisis and the total and conspicuous collapse of the political system, must be interpreted as the first fatal convulsion of the Soviet Empire, the first stage of decay in the entire Eastern bloc.

Jacek Kuron, Solidarity leader in a message from prison in May 1982

The crisis that developed in Poland in 1981 was a general economic crisis that affected not only the food-supply sector. Virtually nothing functioned any longer. Industrial production was reduced catastrophically. Hospitals could no longer obtain the medicines and equipment they needed. Families with small children found it difficult to obtain fresh milk or even powdered milk for their babies.

What is happening today in Poland is quite simply the breakdown of a socialist system. Production and distribution are so severely disturbed that basic needs cannot be satisfied. As early as the late 1970s, in fact, shipments of aid from abroad were required and were mobilized.

In the early 1920s the world's first socialist state, the Soviet Union, sorely needed and received extensive foreign relief from all over the world, and millions of lives were saved thereby. In the early 1980s another socialist state, Poland, in a similar situation needed and received extensive foreign relief.

Such organizations as the Red Cross and Save the Children took the lead, and the general preparedness to help was so great that these organizations were flooded with gifts. During the first nine months of 1982, no less than 325,000 parcels of food, clothing, and other necessities were shipped from Sweden to disaster areas.

The fact that Polish shortages and needs were nearly always interpreted as results of some kind of natural disaster gave an extra incentive to the foreign community's willingness to help. And quite apart from the real causes of the crisis, the need was a real one. Even if it were understood that those who suffered were victims of a disaster which they themselves had helped to bring about, it would not alter the fact that relief was needed. What is hoped for Poland is that the socialist system will eventually be replaced by a better one that will employ the nation's rich resources to its advantage and will enable it to manage without extensive relief shipments from abroad.

Chapter 4

Romania

> Man alone has the power to convert a minus into a plus.
>
> *Alfred Adler,* Austrian psychiatrist, 1928

The Romanian Crisis and Its Roots

> History will demonstrate the inherent superiority of socialism.
>
> *Karl Marx,* 1848

Romania, with a population of 22 million people, 2 million of them in the capital city of Bucharest, has substantial private agriculture: 15 percent of the cropland, half of the cows, and a third of the pigs are to be found in the private sector. Private agriculture, in fact, produces half the eggs, potatoes, and fruit and 40 percent of the meat and vegetables sold in the markets. The rest comes from the collective farms.

The peasants in Romania—like their brothers in other socialist countries—have suffered from an agrarian policy that has systematically destroyed the entrepreneurial environment by killing the incentives to produce. The inevitable consequence of such a policy, a shortage of food, was first noted on a large scale in 1977. In August of that year 35,000 miners went on strike against poor working conditions and the shortage of food, primarily meat. It should be noted that this situation developed in an old agrarian country that was once—like Russia and Poland—one of Europe's granaries.

During the first years of shortage, the groups in power managed to satisfy the need for food by securing large foreign loans and imports, a policy that brought temporary relief but solved nothing. For the next few years the government pursued an opportunistic line of least resistance, while difficulties continued to accumulate. The poor harvests of 1980 and 1981, combined with declining imports, created an acute food crisis.

In January 1981 President Nicolae Ceausescu addressed the problem in a public speech. In accordance with the accepted political pattern, he, the man primarily responsible for the policy that had created the crisis, blamed political subordinates within the agricultural administration for the crop failures, for the low yields, for poor organization, and for taking inadequate responsibility. A month later, however, he was forced to admit that Romanian agriculture had been seriously neglected—a self-criticism without precedent. At the same time, he was obliged to promise a plan for "revolutionizing" the agrarian policy within the period from 1981 to 1985.

Despite the promises, the period began with yet another crop failure and such an acute shortage that basic foodstuffs had to be rationed. In such situations, people are inclined to hoard, thereby intensifying the shortage. Of course, the regime saw the opportunity to blame the shortage on the hoarders, threatening them with imprisonment of up to five years. In order to appease public anger and disappointment, a scapegoat had to be found, and Angelo Miculescu, minister of agriculture, was dismissed in September of 1981.

While Poland is suffering from the most severe economic crisis within the Eastern bloc, Romania is running a close second. The Swedish journalist Richard Swartz submitted the following report from Romania during the winter of 1981–1982:

This is the most trying winter we have experienced since the war. We freeze, many of us do not have enough to eat. Pessimism dominates all private conversations in Romania. People are very critical and take a dark view of the future, but in loyalty to Romanian traditions the great majority swallow their anger—here is none of the political agitation that characterized the situation in Poland long before August 1980. Dissatisfaction appears, in fact, to find an outlet in the lines, longer than ever and forming as soon as a delivery of goods reaches a shop. As a rule—just as in the Soviet Union—the capital city of Bucharest is much better stocked than the provinces. Everybody prepared to get up at dawn and stand in lines for several hours, with a bit of luck, even can obtain some meat.[13]

In a later article Swartz reported on the more insidious roots of the Romanian problem—a stranglehold of dictatorial nepotism practiced by the Ceausescu family:

The cracks in the facade have made continuously more of the reality behind it visible and, thereby, the regime more vulnerable. By means of extensive political purges Ceausescu has tried to plaster the facade and conserve his own monopoly of power. Lately more and more power has openly been concentrated into the hands of the family. Nicolae Ceausescu is Secretary General of the Party, president and Supreme Commander of the Army. His wife, Elena, is First Deputy Prime Minister and Chairman of a Party Commission for State and Party officials and functionaries (in practice an omnipotent staff manager). The son, Nicu, is Chairman of the Youth Section of the Party; the sister of Elena, Alexandria Gainuse, is Deputy Prime Minister and member of the Executive Committee of the Party; the brother of Elena, Gheorghe Petrescu, is Deputy Prime Minister and Minister of Industry. Among the brothers of Nicolae Ceausescu some more Deputy Prime Ministers are to be found, while some high officials such as Manea Manescu, Ion Ionita, and Janos Fazekas all through family ties are bound to the clan Ceausescu.[14]

Romanian Price Policy

A government that robs Peter to pay Paul can, as a rule, calculate with the support of Paul.

George Bernard Shaw, 1925

Following traditional socialist patterns, food prices in Romania were kept stable for decades, a stability possible to achieve only at the cost of steadily increasing state subsidies. At last bread became cheaper than fodder grain, and, as in Poland, the government was forced to resort to brutal punishment to stop peasants from feeding bread to livestock.

It is against this background that the bitter medicines the Romanian people were forced to swallow in February 1982—price increases of 50 to 100 percent on all basic foods—must be seen. It can hardly be mere accident that prices were raised as drastically in Poland the same month.

In accordance with the usual socialist policy, Romanian consumers had been given cheap food at the expense of the producers. The rise in consumer prices was a step in the right direction in that it curbed luxury consumption, but it was not sufficient as a remedial measure. The exploitative prices paid to the peasants had to be substantially increased as well in order to stimulate production.

Higher producer prices, in fact, were promised in January 1982, and some months later the promises were fulfilled. The decisive question, however, is whether the increases were large enough to give the peasants strong incentives to increase production. All too often in the past, government promises of better conditions for the peasants have been mere phrases.

Romanian Loan Policy

Politics is not an exact science.

Otto von Bismarck, 1863

Since the early 1960s, Romania pursued a distinctively independent policy toward the Soviet Union, played on the nationalist strings, and refused to integrate the country's economy into that of the Eastern bloc. After the debilitating food shortages of the past few years and the ever-growing need for foreign aid, not much remains of that independent posture. The fact that during the decade from 1972 to 1982 Romania was the only Warsaw Pact member of the International Monetary Fund (IMF) is relevant. Its principal motive for joining was a desire to be able to draw on the extensive loan capacity of the IMF. From 1972 to early 1982 Romania received credits of $1.3 billion; that borrowing was followed in the summer of 1982 by a promise of an additional $1.5 billion. As a condition of this loan, however, the IMF demanded a radical reorganization of the economic policy that led to the crisis; its demands included the price increases described earlier.

Today Romania, like Poland, has exhausted almost all its potential credit abroad. At the beginning of 1982 its total debt to the West amounted to more than $10 billion, a debt that carries payment obligations the country cannot possibly meet. In recent years, Romania has become notorious in foreign trade for slow and missed payments, and in September 1981—six months later than Poland—this socialist country reached the end of the credit road and had to request respites. In July 1982 a new and similar request had to be made concerning payment obligations of $2 billion, and in 1983 further requests followed. Earlier the country had been able to meet its payment commitments by means of new loans. When this fountain dried up, a liquidity crisis was inevitable. In reality, the crisis meant national bankruptcy, even if none of the lending banks and countries wanted an official declaration of default.

For a country in which both production and consumption are adapted to a continuous supply of loan-financed import goods, a cessation of credit must have severe consequences. Imports must be reduced to a volume that can be paid for by the country's own exports, and since the production of export goods is hampered by stopped deliveries of fuel, raw materials, semimanufactures, and spare parts, the reduction must be drastic.

Since Romania's own oil production—from very rich resources— satisfied less than half its needs, production of energy suffered a severe shock when oil imports, even those from the Soviet Union, were reduced. As a consequence, the supply of electricity had to be cut off for several hours a day.

In the spring of 1982 the Romanian leaders declared that in the future the country must tighten its belt, stand on its own feet, and dispense with foreign borrowing for investments. Since the potential credits abroad were exhausted, the leaders were in fact making a virtue of necessity.

Nevertheless, at the end of 1983 no change for the better could be discerned. Most basic foodstuffs and commodities were rationed, but not even the relatively small rations could be delivered. The lines outside the stores were longer than ever, and many people went hungry.

Chapter 5

Czechoslovakia

> None of the evils which totalitarianism claims to cure are
> worse than totalitarianism itself.
>
> *Albert Camus,* 1956

Sooner or Later a Crisis Must Come

> For a Communist, borrowing from capitalists is similar to the case
> of a Christian selling his soul to the devil.
>
> *Vasil Bilak,* Czech Party Secretary, 1981

In Czechoslovakia, with its 15 million inhabitants, 1.2 million of whom
live in the capital city of Prague, private agriculture has been forcibly
reduced and is today of little significance. After having been forbidden
for thirty years, however, "kolkhoz markets"—free markets in which
the peasants may sell the surpluses from their private plots—were permitted to function again in April 1982. At the same time, the possibilities
for people to lease private plots with areas up to an acre were extended.
These ideological retreats were obvious symptoms of a developing crisis.

After the Communist takeover in 1948, Czech agriculture was socialized and converted into state and collective farms. After a difficult transition period, food production eventually seemed to develop more or less satisfactorily. The political leaders in Czechoslovakia seemed to have greater awareness of the agrarian producers' need for incentives than did their colleagues in most of the other socialist countries, which accounts for the fact that for a long period Czechoslovakia had sufficient food supplies.

But the agricultural policy was still a socialist policy under which the peasants were an outgroup, and sooner or later such a policy is bound to weaken their incentives to produce and pave the way for a food-supply crisis. In Czechoslovakia, this did not happen until 1976 after a poor harvest, a setback that was interpreted as temporary and was, of course, blamed on the weather. The failure was so serious, however, that a scapegoat had to be sacrificed, and in September 1976 the minister of agriculture, Bohuslav Vecera, was forced to resign.

To some extent, those in power learned lessons from the setback and granted the peasants more favorable conditions than they had enjoyed earlier, so much more favorable that production and supply were sufficient for five more years. But in 1981 a poor harvest produced a new crisis, and this one could not be waved aside as a temporary setback on account of bad weather. A new deal in agricultural policy was obviously called for. In February 1982 food prices were increased substantially— the prices of such basic foodstuffs as meat and rice as much as 100 percent. Was it mere accident that these price increases came at the same time as similar price increases in Poland and Romania?

Czechoslovakia was also struck by chain reactions to crises in neighboring countries. Deliveries of electricity from Romania were discontinued, and shipments of coal from Poland were substantially reduced. By the end of 1981, the price of fuel oil had to be raised 75 percent and gasoline 20 percent, and both electricity and gasoline had to be rationed to some extent.

Despite the fact that 1981 in Czechoslovakia was the poorest year since 1948, a year in which crop failure was so severe that reorganization of the economic policy was necessary, the Czechoslovakian government refused to relax the strict central control to the extent that it had been relaxed in Hungary, for example. And two-thirds of Czechoslovakia's foreign trade still takes place within the Communist Council for Mutual Economic Assistance (Comecon), the common market of the Soviet bloc.

In one respect Czech policy differs from that of most of the other socialist countries: the Czechs have refused to resolve their crises and relieve their shortages by foreign borrowing. At the beginning of 1982, Czechoslovakia's debt to the Western world amounted to $3 billion, a decidedly smaller debt than those of most other socialist countries.

"Socialism with a Human Face"

Communism is itself the most successful variant of fascism, fascism with a human face.

Susan Sontag, 1982

Bitter memories from 1968 have much to do with the refusal of the Czech government to relax the bonds of dictatorship that bind the industry and the people of Czechoslovakia. In spite of the high degree of industrial development inherited by the Communist regime when it took over in 1948, industrial production failed to live up to expectations. By the end of the 1960s, dissatisfaction over economic stagnation was growing, and the demand for a radical revision of Czech economic policy led to a palace revolution in January 1968 in which Antonin Novotny, party secretary general since 1957, was deposed and replaced by Alexander Dubcek.

The new leaders tried to stimulate production by following a policy of liberalization, in reality implying some degree of desocialization. The new policy was enthusiastically described by its domestic advocates—and foreign sympathizers—with such expressions as "democratic social-ism" and "socialism with a human face." The socialist leaders in both Yugoslavia and Romania in different ways expressed their sympathies for the new regime and its economic policy. The men in power in the Soviet Union soon realized, however, that the new economic policy in Czechoslovakia could hardly be interpreted as a new version of socialism (like that in Yugoslavia), but meant instead a retreat from and abandon-ment of socialism. When the new Czech government refused, in spite of severe diplomatic Soviet pressures, to change its course, Soviet forces invaded Czechoslovakia in August 1968—following a policy later called the Brezhnev doctrine. The Soviet forces were supported by Bulgarian, Polish, Hungarian, and East German troops, but not by any Romanian troops. The Czech brothers who had gone astray were quickly brought back into the socialist fold, while the prisons were filled with political opponents and dissidents, many of whom are still there.

When the 1968 experiment with democratic socialism in Czecho-slovakia failed, the failure was, in fact, not accidental. Without force, no socialist blueprint or system can be put into practice. All dreams of democratic socialism are—and always will be—as utopian as the dreams of "socialism with a human face." Trying to make democratic socialism function is like trying to balance a pyramid on its tip.

Chapter 6

Yugoslavia

> Among present-day socialist countries, only Yugoslavia can be labeled as next to democratic.
>
> *C. H. Hermansson,* Former Chairman of the Swedish Communist Party, 1981

Crisis with Retarded Release

> We are suffering from serious economic shortcomings and it is high time for a reconstruction of the economic policy. Many people have not yet realized the depth of the abyss we are approaching.
>
> *Lazar Mojsov,* Chairman of the Yugoslavian Communist Party, 1981

In Yugoslavia, a country with a population of 22 million, 800,000 of whom live in the capital of Belgrade, private agriculture clearly dominates. When the Communist Party under Tito assumed power after World War II, all estates and larger farms were socialized without compensation to their owners and were either amalgamated into large state farms or divided up into small farms. Outside the state farms, agriculture was later "voluntarily" consolidated into collective farms following the Soviet model.

For various reasons a political separation from the Soviet Union under Stalin took place in 1948, and after that time Yugoslavia pursued its own course. As a consequence, the Soviet socialist model was abandoned both in agriculture and in industry. Agriculture was desocialized. In 1951 the collective farms were dissolved and the original small farms were, after certain adjustments, returned to their former owners. The large state farms were preserved alongside a system of private small farms, each having a maximum of 10 hectares of cropland. After this revision of the system, 4 million peasants owned 85 percent of the cropland and 90 percent of the livestock.

Following a 1950 law concerning workers' councils, the industrial enterprises that had been socialized were reorganized as employee-controlled corporations—another radical departure from the Soviet model. The new system is in principle decentralized, but the Communist party (with 2 million members) has never released its grip on the economy. Today about 95 percent of the members of the workers' councils are members of the party, which means that the real differences between the Soviet and the Yugoslavian systems are far less in practice than in theory.

As described earlier, socialists in power are obsessed with providing cheap food for their political supporters—the industrial and urban populations—and as a rule they do it at the expense of the peasants. In Yugoslavia low prices were set, but not as low as in the Soviet Union and Poland, for example. Because of comparatively better prices, the supply of food was for many years decidedly better in Yugoslavia than in most other socialist countries. For a number of years, tourists who visited Yugoslavia returned home with reports of a "prosperous" country, in which the stores were well filled. In spite of this, however, the income of the peasants remained lower than it would have been if the markets had been free, so the peasants were in effect deprived of funds that would have enabled them to modernize their farms in the same way as their colleagues in the West had been able to do. Almost a third of the population is still employed in agriculture, a share characterizing Yugoslavia as a less developed country.

The shortage of food that is bound to develop sooner or later in socialist countries was postponed for some years in Yugoslavia, but it came eventually. In 1979 affluence gave way to shortages of food and other commodities, a crisis which has since grown steadily worse, with longer and longer lines outside the stores. The country that before World War II was a granary with substantial surpluses for export is today unable to feed its own people. Even in Yugoslavia, socialism has once again demonstrated its capacity to convert a plus into a minus.

The present general economic crisis in Yugoslavia has demonstrated clearly the shortcomings of the socialist system. Despite the fact that approximately one million Yugoslavians have escaped from unemployment at home and today work abroad, between 12 and 15 percent of the remaining labor force was unemployed in 1982, the highest rate of unemployment in any European country at that time. Another dismal record held by Yugoslavia is deterioration of the currency: In 1980 and 1981, the annual rate of inflation was 40 percent, while in 1982 it had descended to "only" 35 percent.

The seriousness of the crisis is demonstrated by the fact that the standard of living during 1979 to 1983 is reported to have sunk by more than 25 percent. In October 1982 the crisis had become so severe that as winter approached, still further belt-tightening was necessary. Drastic measures were taken in the rationing of gasoline and electricity, and it was announced that people had to be satisfied with less fuel and lower temperatures in their homes. Commodities such as coffee and detergents were rationed, too.

Credit Withdrawal Pains

> Those whom the gods would destroy, they first make overlend, then make overrestrict, then make protectionist.
>
> *The Economist,* August 7, 1982

Yugoslavia has succumbed to the same temptation as have many other socialist welfare states—and many capitalist welfare states as well; it has met the urgent demand for more capital for investment and for public welfare by borrowing extensively abroad. In 1983 its debts to the Western world alone amounted to $20 billion, making Yugoslavia second only to Poland as the most debt-ridden country of Eastern Europe.

More than a third of the country's shrinking export income, including income from its booming tourist industry—more than 5 million tourists a year visit Yugoslavia from the West and 800,000 from the East —had in 1982 to be allocated to the growing debt-service obligation, a burden too heavy to be carried without new loans. Like Romania among the Warsaw Pact countries, Yugoslavia has become a member of the International Monetary Fund—to all appearances, a favored member because of its independence. In February 1982 Yugoslavia was able to cash the second third of a record IMF loan of $2.2 billion that had been granted in January 1981.

As a condition of its generosity, however, the IMF demanded a policy of strict austerity in order to stop the great deficits in foreign trade and to control the galloping inflation. The devaluation of the dinar by 30 percent in 1980 and another 20 percent in 1982, together with numerous restrictions on imports, must be seen against this background. In a report dated March 1982 the IMF praised the country for its decisive austerity and stabilization policies. The IMF, however, is an exception in the credit markets, and by 1982 Western sources of credit had largely dried up.

Yugoslavian industry had become dependent on generous supplies of fuel oil, gasoline, raw materials, semimanufactures, and spare parts from the West. The drastic import restrictions of 1982 meant disaster for industry. A large number of projects that had already been initiated had to be discontinued.

One highly appreciated privilege of Yugoslavian citizens had been the right to travel freely abroad and to import commodities duty-free upon their return. In a desperate effort to favor essential imports at the expense of those considered nonessential, in March 1981 the government reduced the value of what could be imported duty-free to $200 and in December 1981 to the trifling amount of $5.

Is Yugoslavia a Socialist State?

In practice Yugoslavia has gone further along the road to capitalism than any other socialist country.

Paul Sweezy, American Marxist economist, 1969

Yugoslavia is often cited as a country apart from other Communist countries, a country that has nearly achieved "democratic socialism." It is seen, too, as a comparatively free country, although it has had the greatest number of political prisoners in Eastern Europe.[15]

But it is not uncommon to ignore the essence of a system because the system's more superficial features do not conform with one's perceptions of what that essence should be. The majority of socialists outside the Eastern bloc today, for instance, find developments within the Soviet Union so repellent that they repudiate its socialist status—a surprising position to take with respect to a country that has a centrally controlled, state-owned industry and presents a classic example of a socialist economy. Less surprising is the fact that many "orthodox" socialists deny the socialist status of Yugoslavia, pointing to its private agriculture and its employee-controlled enterprises working in some sort of a market economy. According to economist Paul Sweezy:

> The market is the deciding factor in the capitalist economy and by socialism is meant a society which replaces the blind rule of the market with a conscious control of production. Those who work to strengthen the market's influence instead of struggling against it, work—whatever their aims may be—for capitalism and not for socialism.[16]

Chapter 7

Hungary

> A political regime filling the prisons with critics and dissidents is, in reality, a weak regime.
>
> *János Kádár,* Secretary General of the Communist Party, 1964

An Agricultural System That Works

> Real socialism cannot develop without people's creative powers being released.
>
> *György Aczel,* Chairman of the Central Committee, 1982

Hungary, with its 11 million inhabitants, more than 2 million of whom live in the capital city of Budapest, presents a unique picture among socialist countries: The stores are full of food and commodities, and no lines are to be seen. With its fertile soil, Hungary was created by nature for agriculture and has always been one of Europe's breadbaskets. It is, in fact, still producing surpluses for export. What is unique is that the Communists, in taking over the government of Hungary, did not manage to convert this plus into a minus.

In 1957 and 1958 agriculture was socialized and organized into collective farms. As in the Soviet Union, the socialist predilection for largeness brought about continuous amalgamations into larger and larger farms.

A decisive difference between the agrarian economy of Hungary and that of other socialist countries can be seen in the fact that the Hungarian peasants were never treated as an outgroup, as natural objects for exploitation. From the very beginning, the peasants were offered prices that reflected market demand and wages equivalent to those of industrial workers.

The Secret of the Hungarian Exception

> Supporting entrepreneurship and enterprise is the new road to growth. Economic efficiency generally and profitability especially must be strengthened, if our position as an export nation is to be maintained.[17]
>
> *Reszö Nyers,* 1982

When Hungary was taken over by the Communists after World War II, as a matter of course they pursued an economic policy that followed the Soviet model. The result—as in many other states of the Eastern bloc—was economic stagnation and decidedly poor results in both industry and agriculture. In 1956 deep dissatisfaction with the regime at last exploded in a revolt, and the rebels initially were the victors; they took power and held it for a couple of weeks. On November 4 the country was invaded by Soviet forces, however, and approximately 13,000 people were killed. About 200,000 members of the resistance movement were forced to flee the country. The leader of the revolt, Imre Nagy, was executed in 1958. After the revolt, a new leader, János Kádar, Secretary General of the party and prime minister, emerged, and he was initially considered a traitor by the majority of Hungarians. But with such mottoes as "He who is not against us is with us" and "You can be a good Hungarian without being a Communist," Kádar adopted a policy of reconciliation. Taking a less doctrinaire policy position, he eventually reversed public opinion and became a respected father figure.

For more than a decade, however, the Kádar regime continued the earlier Soviet-style policy, with a series of disappointments and failures as the result. When, despite hard work and sincere endeavors, success eluded them, the leaders of the country finally concluded that a new policy was the only medicine that could cure the country's economic disease. In 1968 the political and economic course of Hungary was radically changed.

The new policy, with its extensive investment in private enterprise and, above all, its creation of strong economic incentives, meant a retreat from orthodox socialism. The earlier negative attitude toward private agriculture was changed, and both peasants and city dwellers were encouraged to acquire and cultivate plots of their own. Today there are in Hungary about 1,600,000 private mini-farms, cultivating 6 percent of the cropland—twice as much as in the Soviet Union. In this private sector, more than a third of the food supply is produced. Before the new policy was introduced, both the collective farms and the state farms were objects of detailed central control through planned targets. Now all the farms, like private farms in market economies, are allowed to determine their own product mix, with maximum profits as their target.

If such a system is to function efficiently, realistic prices based on market supply and demand are an absolute requisite, and such a price policy has in fact been pursued in Hungary since 1968. Today those in power in Hungary seem to be almost the only socialist leaders in the world who realize the importance of an entreprenurial environment with strong production incentives, not only for industry but also for agriculture.

Tolerance of private enterprise has increased steadily since 1968, and since 1982 private enterprises having ten to twelve employees have been allowed. Private family collectives and private cooperatively organized firms may have as many as thirty employees.

As a matter of fact, in Hungary today a system is followed similar to that which prevails in New York and Hong Kong, where, for example, taxi licenses are auctioned off to the highest bidder. In Hungary, the right to run private restaurants and other enterprises are auctioned off to the highest bidder. Prices as high as $100,000 a year have been noted.

The secret of the success of the Hungarian economy may be interpreted as a simulation of a free market economy by means of central control and planning. Fundamental to such a policy must be realistic prices that are adapted to markets; during recent years, Hungarian prices have been radically increased in several stages.

What is surprising is that Soviet reaction has been so positive toward

Hungary. Ironically, in his speech to the Soviet Communist Party Congress in March 1981, Brezhnev pointed to Hungary's agricultural policy as a model to be copied by other socialist states.

Borrowing Policy and Debts

> Establishing a realistic value of our currency will make our enterprises more efficient and profitable. Marx, in fact, never argued against profits—only against private profits.
>
> *János Fekete,* President of the Hungarian Central Bank, 1981

In November 1981 Hungary applied for membership in the International Monetary Fund, without any opposition from the Soviet Union. In May 1982 the application was approved, making Hungary the third member, after Romania and Yugoslavia, among the socialist states of Europe.

The positive attitude of the IMF toward Hungary is, to be sure, a consequence of Hungary's economic policy. The fact that in July 1982 Hungary was elected a member of the World Bank may also be attributable to the new economic policy. With debts to the West amounting to nearly $8 billion, Hungary has, in fact, heavy debt-service burdens to carry—35 percent of its export income, an even higher proportion than Romania's 25 percent. Without new credits, Hungary would be unable to fulfill its obligations.

The possibilities for Hungary to obtain new credits are sharply limited, however, since the private sources have dried up. From the Bank for International Settlements (BIS), a cooperative institute for the Western Central Banks, Hungary received in October 1982 a standby credit of $300 million, giving the country a respite of six months. The liquidity situation is strained, and the country's hope is focused on a large, long-term credit from the IMF. According to János Fekete, president of the Central Bank, chain reactions of difficulties threaten to develop if the Western banks are too restrictive in granting new credits.

Even though Hungary's indebtedness per capita is greater than Poland's, the country has done its utmost to fulfill its debt-service obligations and, in 1983, succeeded in these efforts—partly due to new credits. Whether these obligations can be fulfilled in the future is an open question.

In spite of its heavy indebtedness, Hungary's economic situation is decidedly stronger than that of most of the other socialist countries. While large shares of the loans in these countries have been used for consumption, the greater part of the loans to Hungary has been invested in profitable enterprises.

The country's economic strength has been demonstrated conspicuously by the fact that in recent years it has opened its borders to about 10 million tourists a year from the East, visitors who buy as much as possible from well-filled Hungarian stores. Similarly, three million tourists a year have been pouring in from the West. Three hundred thousand Hungarians a year are permitted to travel to the West, a stream from which an average of 3 percent do not return, a loss obviously looked upon as acceptable by Hungarian authoritries.

The monetary unit of Hungary, the forint, has grown steadily stronger, and it appears to be only a question of time before it becomes the first completely convertible currency in the socialist sphere. Under the new economic policy, balance in foreign trade is an important goal, which the government hopes to achieve primarily by means of export incentives and realistic exchange rates. In trying to keep the borders to the West open, they try as far as possible to avoid protectionist measures. By this market-oriented new policy, Hungary has been able to achieve the highest standard of living among socialist countries.

In spite of all "liberal" reforms Hungary is, however, still a socialist state with a socialist economy, an economy bound to produce, sooner or later, problems and stagnation. Earlier development has, in fact, recently been followed by several years of stagnation.

In April 1984, the Central Committee of Hungary's Communist Party took new steps toward economic liberalization: further wage and price decontrol and further decentralization of management. These measures may be interpreted as desperate efforts to start a new expansion.

In the 1956 revolution, the aim of the rebels was not to abandon socialism but, primarily, to achieve political and economic independence from the Soviet Union. Their effort to cut the bonds failed, however. With 60,000 of its soldiers stationed in the country, the Soviet Union still holds Hungary in a firm grip.

Chapter 8

Portugal

> Socialism is like a dream. Sooner or later you wake up to reality.
>
> *Winston Churchill,* 1938

The Socialist Revolution in 1974 and Later

> The more conspicuously the easternizing of Western Europe is advancing, the more vehemently it is denied.
>
> *Rita Tornborg,* Swedish author, 1982

When in 1974 the almost fifty-year-old Portuguese dictatorship was overthrown by a military revolt, a provisional government, initially Communist-dominated, took power. Strong internal tensions among competing groups led to a highly unstable situation, virtually paralyzing the government and bringing about a condition that closely resembles anarchy. Encouraged and supported by the Communists, the agricultural workers saw their opportunity in this situation and occupied most of the large estates in the estate-dominated provinces of southern Portugal, especially in the Allentejo province. The owners were driven off their land and often were not even permitted to take their personal belongings with them. The estates were divided up and converted into worker-controlled collective farms. At the end of 1975 there were 550 such farms, covering 1,500,000 hectares of cropland. Approximately 100,000 people, including members of the families, lived on them and cultivated them.

In the 1976 election—the first free election in fifty years—the "social democratic" Socialist party received 35 percent of the vote, the "liberal" Social Democratic party 25 percent, and the Moscow-oriented Communist party 15 percent. The result was a great disappointment to the earlier dominant group of Communists, who were now out of power. Mario Soares, the leader of the Socialist party, became premier in the new government.

This government, and several subsequent governments as well, tried to recover the illegally occupied estates and return them to their owners. But the occupiers, supported by the Communists, stubbornly defended their captured property, and by 1983 fewer than 25 percent of the estates had been returned.

Unlike private farmers, members of the occupied collectives were in the privileged position of having "received" their property free of charge. In spite of the privilege, however, they were usually short of capital to purchase machines, seed, and chemical fertilizers and to pay wages, but the government at first reacted favorably to their pleas for help and generously met their demands for loans. It was assumed that the collective farms would not only be able to manage themselves after the first crop had been harvested, but that they would also be able to repay the loans—an assumption that would prove to be incorrect.

The production of the collective farms soon turned out to be so poor that the income usually did not even suffice to pay the minimum wages set by the socialist government. The poor harvests, in accordance with traditional socialist practice, were attributed to bad weather year after year, and the farms could hobble along only with the help of new loans and an increased debt. When the governments tightened the reins and withdrew credits, many of the collective farms went into bankruptcy, unable to pay wages, buy seed, or repair machinery, and they were of course unable to buy fertilizers or new machines. More and more of the cropland was laid fallow. Only in 1979 in the Allentejo province was an effort made to improve the situation— about a million hectares of farmland were converted into hunting grounds.

A system of worker-controlled enterprises is very often labeled a system of economic democracy, and because of that the Portuguese experiment is of historical significance. The conclusion to be drawn from the experiment is that worker-controlled farms seem to function even worse than state-controlled farms in the Soviet Union and other socialist countries.

A Socialist Shortcut to a Severe Economic Crisis

Politicians work energetically to solve problems they themselves create.

Assar Lindbeck, Swedish economist, 1977

After the election victory of 1976, the socialist government with Premier Mario Soares at the helm took full advantage of the opportunity to carry out a socialist economic revolution. Most of the bank capital was confiscated when the banks, the insurance companies, and the great industrial corporations were socialized. In this hostile entrepreneurial environment, many private companies were threatened with bankruptcy, so takeovers by the government were judged necessary in order to prevent increases in unemployment.

Following the traditional socialist policy of favoring the industrial and urban population with cheap food, the government set prices of agricultural products so low that the inevitable occurred. The private peasants in central and northern Portugal and the collective peasants in southern Portugal found themselves with only weak incentives to produce.

Before the 1974 revolution, exports and imports of agricultural products were roughly in balance; the country could feed itself. After 1974, the situation deteriorated rapidly. Exports were reduced and imports increased to such an extent that after only a few years half of the country's food had to be imported, a proportion later increased to 60 percent. This collapse of agricultural production took place in an old agricultural country in which before 1974 cropland had amounted to 25 percent of the total land area (in the United States the percentage is 20).

The miraculous ability of a socialist government to convert a plus into a minus had been demonstrated again.

The imports of large volumes of food consumed such a high proportion of the shrinking export income that the country—despite extensive foreign borrowing—had growing difficulty in financing the import of other necessities. In 1978, when the country at last was able to harvest a good potato crop, transportation between producers and consumers was hampered by a severe shortage of gasoline and other motor fuels. While Portuguese consumers cried for food, many of the potatoes rotted in the fields. The successive failures of socialist policy drove the sympathies of the electorate from left to right. The setback suffered by the Communist party during the first election of 1976 was significant. After a socialist election setback in 1978, caused by growing discontent due to the steadily intensifying economic crisis, the socialist government under Mario Soares was forced to resign.

The various coalition governments, usually with the Social Democrats as one party that held power from 1978 to 1983, functioned as weak "welfare governments," unable to change the socialist course in any decisive way. The result was a bad economic situation that grew worse year after year. Both oppression and exploitation of private entrepreneurs in agriculture and industry and mismanagement of socialized enterprises were responsible for setbacks in production and supply and a rapidly growing rate of unemployment. According to official reports, inflation in Portugal in the 1980s has fluctuated between 20 and 30 percent and unemployment between 10 and 15 percent.

In spite of enormous imports of food, financed largely by foreign loans, the country's requirements could not be met, and in 1982 lines appeared outside the stores, the most obvious symptom of an acute shortage of the basics. In February 1982 a half-million people, with the largest trade union—Communist-controlled—in the lead, demonstrated on Lisbon's main street, the Avenida da Liberdade, against shortages and hardships and against the austere policies of the nonsocialist government. Social unrest, manifested in strikes and demonstrations, was never greater in Portugal. In the southwestern corner of Europe, Portugal was on its way to becoming another Poland.

Although interest payments on the foreign debt—rapidly growing from $10 billion in 1982 to $13 billion in 1983—consume 25 percent of the national budget, the government considers more borrowing its only hope. In the face of the acute economic crisis, however, lenders are becoming less and less willing—and not without reason. "The truth is that we no longer can fulfill our debt obligations—we can only manage the interest," Secretary of State Marcelo Rebelo de Sousa admitted in January 1982.[18] Nevertheless, the "lender of the last resort," IMF, in October 1983 accorded Portugal a new loan of $738 million.

After eight years of socialist policies, the welfare state in Portugal had come to the end of the credit road. The governments had systematically destroyed the entrepreneurial environment and killed production incentives in both agriculture and industry. It had consumed and wasted both domestic capital assets and the potential for new loans from private credit institutions abroad. Future loans from institutions like the International Monetary Fund will be limited and accompanied by strict conditions for following hard austerity policies.

In the April 1983 elections, the Socialist party could successfully exploit the dissatisfaction accumulated during five years of nonsocialist governments, and Premier Soares could as premier form a new government—the fifteenth since 1974—in coalition with the Social Democratic party. But Soares could not escape the need to pursue an austerity policy still more severe than that of the preceding government. He had to start by devaluing the escudo by 12 percent and was forced to continue a radical reduction of food subsidies, a reduction requiring that prices of basic foodstuffs be increased by 25 to 60 percent. The new economic policy pursued by the new government meant a remarkable retreat from earlier socialist policies in Portugal. Private enterprise was allowed in sectors such as banking, insurance, and manufacturing which had been strictly socialized earlier. And they were permitted to lay off redundant labor. It is clear the Soares government realized that their only alternative was national bankruptcy.

The year 1983, with price hikes of 30 percent and living standards down about 10 percent, was a trying one for the Portuguese. The economic situation continued to deteriorate. In March 1984, 600 companies were unable to pay full wages—or any wages at all—and thousands of workers demonstrated in the streets of Lisbon. But most of the workers, aware of the critical situation of business and fearing bankruptcies and unemployment, did not go out on strike.

Chapter 9

China

> In a world in which Russian Communism will have disintegrated by the end of the century, China is going capitalist.
>
> *Arthur Seldon,* British economist, 1981

Economic Developments after 1949

> Socialist revolutions will inevitably involve a gigantic release of productive powers and pave the way for unprecedented growth within agriculture and industry.
>
> *Mao Tse-tung,* 1956

In the three newly industrialized states with Chinese populations—Singapore, Taiwan, Hong Kong—those in power since 1949 have invested primarily in economic freedom—market economies—and these investments have released dynamic creative powers and have initiated rapid expansions generally referred to as economic miracles.

By 1982 the Communist regime in China had been in power for a third of a century, and except for minor conflicts—Korea in 1950, India in 1962, and Vietnam from 1979 forward—it had enjoyed peaceful relations with the outside world. Certainly the opportunity to achieve economic development was afforded in this climate of relative peace.

If the socialist revolution of 1949 had been able to release those miraculous powers spoken of by Mao Tse-tung in 1956 (see epigraph above), the economic performance of China would have exceeded by far those of the free-market economic systems of the three countries mentioned above. Yet China's performance has been poor. Indeed, China can point with pride to the stable price level it succeeded in maintaining throughout the 1960s and 1970s. But less impressive is the stability of the Chinese wage level during the same period, a stability that implies an unchanged standard of living and, therefore, economic stagnation.

The stagnation has, of course, been blamed at various times on the too optimistic "Great Leap" of the early 1960s, on the economic reversals during the Cultural Revolution of 1966–1976, and—after the death of Mao in 1976—on the "Gang of Four." One fact, however, is indisputable: After more than thirty years of socialism, China is still an underdeveloped country. Housing is so poor that two or three families must share a kitchen, and modern facilities are rare; one-fourth of the population is still illiterate; resources are so scarce that education above the elementary school level can be provided for only a few young people; 80 percent of the population work in agriculture, yet the country cannot produce enough food to meet domestic needs. In December 1980 the government was forced to appeal to the world through the United Nations to help them alleviate hunger.

Collectivization and Starvation

> War is not only probable, it is necessary for the triumph of world Communism. In such a war we would be willing to sacrifice three hundred million human lives.
>
> *Mao Tse-tung,* 1963

In 1950, the year following the Communist victory under Mao's leadership, the large estates were confiscated and distributed to the tenants and tillers. The next step in the socialization plan was to amalgamate the small farms into large collective farms, and in 1956 it was reported that 83 percent of the peasants were integrated into such units. These two steps were quite in accordance with the Soviet model. The Mao government, however, saw a third step as necessary, and in 1958 the collective farms were amalgamated into still larger units, the so-called people's communes, gigantic comprehensive enterprises that would be productive not only in agriculture but in all necessary areas—in handicrafts, workshops, manufacturing, and construction.

In an underdeveloped country in which nearly 90 percent of the population was employed in agriculture in 1949, these reforms were not only revolutionary transformations of the social order but changes implying unavoidable conflict with the natural conservatism of the peasants: their wishes to safeguard the established order, including their private property. A revolution against the will of the majority can be carried out by a minority if that minority is in command of the state coercive apparatus—the police, the army, prisons, slave camps, and execution platoons—and is prepared to suppress all opposition with brutal force and terrorism. Mao and his Communist cadres were such a minority. The transformation of Chinese agriculture into gigantic people's communes would have been impossible without brutality and terrorism, and severe crop failures were the consequence.

During the three years of famine, 1959 to 1962, millions starved to death. Official reports were never published, but estimates based on death statistics and population censuses indicate that at least 20 million people died from hunger. Before 1958, when the people's communes were initiated, approximately 7.5 million people a year died in China, but in 1960 the number rose to 17.8 million, an increase of 10.3 million. The worst famine year was 1960, but all three years were trying years.[19]

During these years the Communist party, basing its power on the political support of the industrial and urban population—and therefore identifying itself with these groups—barely succeeded in meeting the needs of the supporting groups by "vacuuming" the rural areas in ruthless confiscation raids and by importing food on a large scale. Starvation, therefore, as it had been in the Soviet Union under Lenin and Stalin, was mainly an affliction of the countryside. The situation was further aggravated by the fact that Mao in his doctrinaire fanaticism for orthodox socialism, had forbidden such remnants of capitalism as private plots and kolkhoz markets. During the famine years, however, Mao was forced to retreat, and both private plots and the free markets in the cities, where the peasants were allowed to sell surpluses from their plots, were declared legal.

But it was a reluctant retreat, and during the Cultural Revolution of 1966–1976, when unorthodox pragmatists and other dissidents were purged, Mao again tried to abolish the remnants of capitalism. This time almost everyone except Mao realized that the private plots were absolutely necessary for the provision of food. Even before Mao's death, the 1975 constitution confirmed the rights of members of the people's communes to cultivate private plots, to devote part of their time to private jobs, and to keep a small number of domestic animals for their personal needs. The plots, in fact, have survived Mao and today a substantial portion of the food supply is produced on them.

Disintegration of the People's Communes

The socialization of agriculture will, according to the Soviet experience, require long time and hard work, but without such socialization there will never be complete and consolidated socialism.

Mao Tse-tung, 1949

In 1958, by which time the collectivization of agriculture had been completed, but before communalization had been undertaken, there were 750,000 producers' cooperatives—as the collective farms were called in China—with an average of 160 households per farm. Like Lenin and Stalin, however, Mao was obsessed by gigantomania, by a naive belief in the advantages of large-scale production. In 1958 the Mao government decided to consolidate the 750,000 collective farms into 26,000 communes.

It was not long, however, before these gigantic enterprises, each with an average of 5,000 households, were found to be unmanageable. They were divided up, and by 1962 the number of communes had increased to 74,000. Mao considered this division a retreat, and during the Cultural Revolution he and the "revolutionaries" enforced new consolidations. In 1980 there were approximately 50,000 people's communes in China.

The realities behind the official facade of the huge people's communes are less well known. Practical work experience soon demanded that the gigantic communes once again be divided, this time into more or less independent units called brigades—units that were later to be divided further into production teams consisting of about twenty households each. After Mao's death in 1976 and the imprisonment of the Gang of Four which included Mao's widow, the process of division continued, and since 1980 the people's communes have disintegrated into their original components, small private farms. This retreat was, to be sure, concealed in many ways. Contracts were signed between the commune and the "private" peasants, who promised to produce certain yearly quantities of grain and to raise a specified number of domestic animals for the commune at prices fixed by the government. As a rule, these contracts were drawn in such a way as to give peasants opportunities to produce surpluses, which they are allowed to sell at free prices on free markets. It is hoped that this system will provide adequate incentives, and so stimulate the peasants to higher production. One of Mao's fundamental mistakes was his assumption that people in socialist enterprises would work without personal economic incentive, stimulated only by an enthusiasm for socialism and notions of public welfare. Nor was it particularly beneficial to economic efficiency that in a society with an eight-grade wage structure, the highest wages were typically paid to managers who had received their posts as rewards for loyal party work and ideological orthodoxy rather than for their occupational training, expertise, and experience.

The disintegration of the people's communes was hastened by obvious inefficiency; they were simply unable to produce sufficient quantities of food. In 1979 it was officially admitted that at least 100 million Chinese suffered from food shortages. In this strained situation, the prices paid to the producers for basic food were raised more than 20 percent, increases expected to stimulate the peasants to higher production. But the food crisis continued, and in 1981, according to official statements, 100 million still suffered shortages close to starvation levels. From 1982 and later, a decided improvement of the supply situation seems to have occurred, most probably a result of the radical economic reforms instituted after the death of Mao.

Some remarkable observations can be made from Chinese agricultural statistics. In 1979 a record grain harvest of 332 million tons was reported, and for the following four years the volumes were 318, 327, 335, and 355 million tons. For all of these years the harvested quantities were so large that if they had actually been produced, there should have been no shortages between 1979 and 1981. But in China—as in the Soviet Union—farm managers have a personal interest in concealing dismal realities behind impressive figures. And in China—as well as in the Soviet Union—it is clearly easier to concoct impressive figures than to produce sufficient quantities of food.

An adverse development under the Communist regime has been the successive reductions in cultivated acreage from 110 million hectares in 1949 to 99 million in 1977. The seriousness of this development can be seen from the fact that while in 1949 there were .20 hectares of cropland per inhabitant in China, by 1977 the area had shrunk to only .10 hectares. Since only 10 percent of the land in China is under cultivation, it seems likely that the Chinese could keep pace with population growth if they opened up new land to cultivation. But for this to happen the social system must offer adequate incentives to the peasants. Apparently no such incentives have existed.

Imports of grain were made necessary by the catastrophic harvest of 1960, which produced only 160 million tons and caused famine. This was generally believed to be only a temporary setback, but the import of grain has continued and increased. In 1978 imports of 9 million tons were reported, and in 1979, despite a record harvest, imports were increased to 12 million tons, a volume that in 1982 had grown to 15 million tons. This volume is modest in comparison with the import of 32 million tons by the Soviet Union in 1979, but it is obvious that the amounts that China imported were not sufficient to meet the urgent needs of the country. China is a poor, underdeveloped country, traditionally unwilling to borrow abroad, and it has not been able to afford the importation of quantities great enough to eliminate shortages.

One reason that funds for import are short is that comprehensive government subsidies are mobilized to keep prices of grain, table oil, and cotton at low levels. When in 1979 producer prices were increased by 20 percent, the major part of the increase to consumers was eliminated by state subsidies. The total cost of these food subsidies was $4.5 billion in 1978, $8.4 billion in 1979, $12 billion in 1980, and $18.4 billion in 1981—expenses that in 1981 consumed at least 20 percent of the national budget. Subsidizing and stimulating consumption in this way in an underdeveloped country as poor as China—rather than directing scarce funds for investment—is contrary to a rational allocation of resources.

Simultaneous with the dissolution of the people's communes in 1981 came the government's disclosure—a remarkable coincidence—that the famous Dazhai commune, which since 1964 had been Mao's model for the whole country, was a fraud. The good reputation of the leaders had been built on falsified production reports, and the peasants had been oppressed in the most brutal manner and had been forbidden to cultivate plots of their own—in contradiction with the official story that the members of this commune had voluntarily agreed out of socialist zeal to refrain from cultivating private "capitalist" plots and thereby dispensing with income from surpluses sold in free markets. In Dazhai as in other communes, the land has now been returned to individual peasant families. How will these revelations be received by those socialists who in pilgrimages to the new promised land of China eagerly visited and enthusiastically greeted the model commune's sanguine reports?

Desocialization of China

The food supply is the fundamental problem. Whether a cat is white or black does not matter. As long as it catches mice, it is a good cat.

Deng Xiaoping, 1978

The continuing dissolution of the people's communes must be interpreted as part of the general desocialization that began in 1976 after Mao's death, a retreat from socialism that has been accelerated during the last few years. In the 1980s growing emphasis was placed on private enterprise in the struggle against unemployment. Private firms having as many as seven employees were permitted to exist, and everyone was encouraged to start his own business.

The constitution by which everyone is granted the right to a job has become a paper law, and young people, especially hard hit by unemployment, are being urged to try to find jobs for themselves. Even in China the high unemployment rate among young people has led to a rise in crime. The activities of private enterprise have been stimulated further by the repeal of job security laws prohibiting dismissal of employees. One consequence of the new policies could be studied in the rapidly growing foreign trade. In 1979 China was Hong Kong's fourteenth largest export market, but in 1982 it was fourth.

A step in the same direction was the establishing in 1978 of four free economic zones in southeastern China, zones in which free-market economies and various privileges are offered those foreign private companies that establish affiliated firms there. In August 1983 it was reported in the *Ren Min Bao* that foreign companies had invested close to $5 billion between 1979 and 1982, of which $1 billion went to offshore industry. According to the same report, China had during the years mentioned received $7.65 billion as credits from abroad. This borrowing indicates a new policy in a country that under Mao had consistently declined offers of "dirty" capital from abroad.

Indicative of this desocialization policy was the fact that Zhao Ziyang, "the magician from Sichuan," was elected prime minister in September 1980. As party head in his home province of Sichuan, with 100 million inhabitants, he had after 1976 led a campaign to liberate industry from various regulations, restrictions, and duties. Sichuan had been the first province in China to dissolve the people's communes. This liberation of enterprise released powers that in a period of three years increased industrial production 81 percent and rice production 25 percent.

The top man in the Chinese power hierarchy since December 1978 is deputy prime minister Deng Xiaoping, eighty in 1984, a typical pragmatist, intent on creating the necessary incentives for individuals to accelerate the engine of production in a country where incentive was killed long ago. That both Deng and Zhao had been banished from their posts during the Cultural Revolution is hardly surprising.

Further evidence of the desocialization process now taking place in China is that advertising is now permitted both in newspapers and on radio and television; that some 43,000 free markets have been opened in the country since 1978—markets in which the peasants may freely sell surpluses not only from private plots but also, after the dissolution of the communes, from family farms; and finally, that since the end of the Cultural Revolution in 1976 order has been restored in the schools, with stern discipline, written tests, and grades at all levels.

Chapter 10

India

> The only chance for development in countries such as India
> is a capitalist agriculture with some welfare elements. I claim
> that, even though I am a Social Democrat.
>
> *Gunnar Myrdal,* 1964

Semisocialism and Stagnation

> India is steadily sinking. According to the World Bank, India no
> longer belongs to the Third World but—together with countries like
> Uganda and Bangladesh—to the miserable Fourth World.
>
> *Jan Myrdal,* 1980

India, with a population of 700 million in 1983, 10 million of whom live
in Calcutta, 8 million in Bombay, and 5 million in the capital city of
New Delhi, became an independent nation in 1947. During the colonial
period, poverty and shortages could be blamed on imperial oppression.
When independence was finally achieved, everyone presumed that
rapid industrial and cultural development would soon follow.

In India's parliamentary democratic system, the political leaders were
elected in universal free elections. During the first thirty years, the
power of government was wielded by the Congress party, and its leader,
Jawaharlal Nehru, was the first prime minister. It is understandable that

a country such as India, which had long been oppressed by a capitalist power, would choose a socialist system when it at last gained independence. But Indian socialism assumed a profile of its own. During the 1960s banks and insurance companies were socialized, and roughly 60 percent of the manufacturing industry is state-owned today. A substantial amount of private enterprise is permitted, however, and some early plans for the collectivization of agriculture were never carried out. On the other hand, prices, wages, production, and trade were to be controlled by the state, which proceeded to place a dead hand on the Indian economy.

According to the 1971 census, 73 percent of the population was still engaged in agriculture—the same proportion as in 1921. And in 1980 two-thirds of the population was still illiterate. Although India has received enormous amounts in foreign aid, economic development has been disappointingly slow. Mass poverty appears to have increased, and the income of 40 to 50 percent of the population is below the subsistence level. In 1980 only 25 percent of the 600,000 villages had access to electricity, and the consumption of paper per capita was less than one hundredth that in the United States.

The caste system, abolished in 1947 and later reabolished several times, is still well established in the Indian society. Something like 105 million Indians remain untouchables and are regarded by the rest of society as inherently inferior. They are probably the largest oppressed minority of the world. Untouchable men are even forbidden from shaping their moustaches upwards—the act would signify an intolerable self-assertion.[20]

Oppression of the Peasants and Semistarvation

Formerly the peasants expected support and relief from their Lord in Heaven. Nowadays they expect support and relief from their Lords in Government.

Otto Järte, Swedish politician, 1933

The socialists in power in India proceeded to oppress the peasants in private agriculture—a sector dominated by small family farms—by means of price controls and compulsory deliveries to state purchasers. As in most socialist countries discussed here, the grain was bought at low procurement prices and sold to consumers at prices made even lower by state subsidies.

The proportion of landless persons in the countryside increased from 22 percent in 1956 to 25 percent in 1980. Dissatisfaction has naturally been strong among the peasants—so strong that many of them have refused to sell to the state purchasers. Discontent has found various outlets. Many families produce just enough to be self-supporting. Others raise more livestock and use surplus grain as fodder. Others sell their surpluses on the black markets that spring up when there are shortages.

As a result of government price policy, the quantities of food bought at low producers' prices have been insufficient, and, since everyone wants to buy food at low, controlled prices, the lines outside the stores have been long. Stocks are quickly exhausted, and those at the end of the lines must buy on the black market, at prices twice as high as those in the stores.

Good harvests alternate with poor ones, but even during the poor years people somehow muddle along. Nevertheless, the years from 1965 to 1967 brought severe crop failures and many starved to death. Even during the good years some food has been imported—mainly in the form of aid shipments—but in India imports have never approached the volumes now required in the Soviet Union. Even if actual starvation is uncommon, undernourishment and severe malnutrition are widespread among the great numbers of poor, both in the countryside and in the city slums.

With an agricultural policy that featured incentive, food production in India, where 50 percent of the land is under cultivation, could have been satisfactory. The government predictably blames the lack of food on poor weather, hoarding, and black-market speculation—the tried and true socialist argument to divert attention from the real villain, the state agricultural policy.

According to reports in the 1980s, in India the political leaders have demonstrated new insights into the necessity of creating better entrepreneurial environments with stronger production incentives, both in agriculture and in the industrial sectors. They also appear to have comprehended that the earlier concentration of resources in manufacturing industry must be replaced by a better balance between manufacturing and agriculture, between the cities and the countryside. One thing is obvious, however: Indian food supply is on the brink of disaster; even a small mistake in agrarian policy could produce catastrophe.

India is the world's largest producer and exporter of tea. In February 1984 the government, in order to win sympathy—and votes—from the domestic tea consumers, introduced a rigid price control combined with an export embargo on tea. This measure is bound to have disastrous consequences for both production and export.

Indira Gandhi, Democracy, and the Future

> Since the State of Emergency was proclaimed in June 1975, some 200,000 people have been imprisoned in India because of their opinions.
>
> *Claes Engström,* Swedish author, 1977

During his last years in power, Nehru, India's first prime minister, was assisted by his daughter Indira, whose married name is Gandhi. In 1966, two years after the death of Nehru, she was appointed prime minister. When the leaders of the Congress party backed her, they hoped that they would be able to retain most of the influence themselves. After only a few years, however, she had gathered the reins of power into her own hands, and from 1969 became the dominant political leader.

It is difficult to preserve law, order, and discipline in a country as enormous as India, and when in 1975 Mrs. Gandhi felt forced to proclaim a state of emergency and place the country under martial law, it was a makeshift measure, difficult to reconcile with a democratic system. Not without reason, she was criticized for abuse of power and for nepotism, criticized so severely and so justly that in 1977, for the first time since 1947, she and her party, the Congress party, lost the elections. After eleven years of political leadership, she was forced to relinquish it. Most people believed that her political career was ended. Mrs. Gandhi herself did not share this belief, however, and after the victory of the Congress party in the next election, held in 1980, she resumed power

—a great personal triumph. Parliamentary democracy in India, the world's largest democracy, had stood the test.

The semisocialist policies followed earlier had not been successful. India's fundamental problems of development and supply were still unsolved, and the earlier optimism had been replaced by deep pessimism. Indira Gandhi's election victory in 1980 gave her a new chance. Would she make full use of it?

She has obviously learned some lessons. Today she seems to be aware of the fact that the earlier concentration on socialized industries was a mistake. Since 1980 a retreat from socialism has taken place, and many restrictions on private enterprise have been removed. The establishment of foreign corporations in India has been facilitated, and, as a consequence, American investment in India has increased by 40 percent. The earlier intimate economic cooperation with the Soviet Union had never produced the industrial "kick" India had hoped for and needed. Mrs. Gandhi's official visit to the United States in 1982 marked a cautious change of economic and political course.

Chapter 11

Vietnam

> A society which maintains that the interest of the individual is negligible compared to the interest of the nation is a lawless society.
>
> *Alexander Zinoviev,* 1979

The Historical Background

> "We shall convert our prisons into schools," the Head of the Communist party in Vietnam, Le Duan, promised after the takeover of the South in 1975, and simple-hearted democrats all over the world cheered.
>
> *Andres Küng,* Swedish author, 1982

In Vietnam, with a population of 50 million, the present capital city of Hanoi has a population of 1.5 million, while Saigon has a population of 3.5 million. The long war ended in the spring of 1975 when Communist-controlled North Vietnam defeated South Vietnam and the American forces and so assumed control over all Vietnam.

Some two decades earlier, in 1954, the war against France, the colonial power, had ended with the defeat of the French in the decisive battle of Dien Bien Phu. The Communists assumed power in North Vietnam, while nonsocialist groups were victorious in South Vietnam. From 1954 to 1975, the country was divided into politically distinct entities.

After taking over North Vietnam in 1954, the Communists socialized the economy and combined the small private farms into large collective farms. This fundamental transformation produced economic disruptions so severe that agricultural production since that time has not been sufficient to feed the country but has had to be supplemented by imports.

A subversive Communist movement, the NLF, initiated guerilla warfare against the regime in the South in 1957; from the beginning, it was supported by the Communist regime in the North. As the revolt spread and gained momentum, Northern support became more extensive, and the United States increased its military support to South Vietnam. Operations soon escalated into a full-scale war, and extensive damage was dealt to all of Vietnam's industry and agriculture.

Agriculture and Food Supply after 1975

Ever since China canceled its Vietnamese development programs in 1978, the Soviet Union has supplied Viet Nam with everything from brandy to ball bearings. After Hanoi invaded neighboring Kampuchea [formerly Cambodia] in 1979 and most Western nations suspended aid, that dependence on Moscow has become near total.

Time, February 12, 1982

The poor yield from the collective farms in the North explains why the Communist regime refrained from socializing agriculture in the South after 1975. The regime did not refrain, however, from using its power to impose price controls. The low procurement prices and the still lower subsidized consumers' prices have greatly contributed to the food shortage. While state shops were selling rice for the equivalent of six cents a pound, prices on the free markets were ten or more times as high.

During recent years the urban population has had to manage with food rations far smaller than those they received during the war years.

In 1981 the low rations were reduced even further, and in 1982 the official rice ration was 24 pounds per month, whereas 33 pounds has always been considered a minimum to prevent serious undernourishment. Even at the reduced amounts, the inhabitants seldom received the official rations.

Nonagricultural production has fallen drastically, too. The shortages of motor fuel and boats—the boat refugees presumably took half the fishing fleet with them—explain the drop in fish catches from 600,000 tons in 1976 to 350,000 tons in 1980. Throughout the country many people, including a preponderance of children, are seriously undernourished. The situation is worst in the North, where the farms have been collectivized. There, half the population is reported to be undernourished.

In spite of strict rationing of rice and other staples, it has been necessary to import food in such extensive volumes that the ports are constantly blocked by grain-carrying ships. The large imports have not been able to offset the shortages, which have been more severe during recent years than they were during the war. Of course the government blames the shortages on poor harvests caused by bad weather. After the poor crop in 1977, the threat of famine was so severe that the government was forced to appeal to "friendly nations" for assistance; another crop failure in 1978 sent it forth with renewed appeals.

Terror and Flight

Communist Vietnam which won the war against the French and later against the Americans is on the verge of losing the peace.

Le Monde, October 17, 1978

The general supply situation in Vietnam certainly did not improve when for ideological reasons the government forbade 30,000 private businessmen in South Vietnam to engage in "private capitalism." Many of them were ethnic Chinese whom the Vietnamese government had driven out of the country in 1978 and 1979 in an effort to eliminate the "Chinese-born bourgeoisie"—a significant cog in "world capitalism," according to the regime. This expulsion, perceived by China as an unfriendly act, was one of the reasons for the punitive action taken by China in February 1979.

The main reason, however, was the Vietnamese invasion of Cambodia in January 1978 and the war against the Red Khmers, a Communist regime supported by the Chinese. The war in Cambodia, which has engaged some 150,000 Vietnamese soldiers and is still raging in 1984, has been costly for Vietnam. Since 1975, Communist Vietnam has continuously kept 700,000 to 1 million men under arms, an unbelievably massive military mobilization of resources by one of the world's poorest countries.

As a consequence of the military adventure in Cambodia—and a small adventure in Laos as well—one of Vietnam's most important supporters and suppliers, China, cut off all deliveries, while the United States canceled its promised reconstruction aid. Even other Western countries ceased giving aid to Vietnam. The sole exception was Sweden, which continued to support the Bai Bang "prestige project," in 1982–1983 with $55 million.

Vietnam is now forced to rely on aid from the Soviet Union, which during recent years pumped some $3 million a day into the country. In addition, 6,000 Soviet experts and advisers were sent to help the regime get the economy back on its feet.

Revolutionary economic transformations such as those in Vietnam, carried out against the will of the majority of the people, can be achieved only through ruthless terrorism. The decree of April 1978 prohibiting private trading and manufacturing caused more than half a million people to leave the country in desperate efforts to escape terror and the threat of starvation and death. To these figures must be added a further half million from Cambodia and Laos. In April 1983, 840,000 had arrived in new home countries, of whom 493,000 went to the United States, 88,000 to France, 86,000 to Canada, and 74,000 to Australia. Most of these escaped as boat refugees. Another 275,000 escaped over the borders to China, while 150,000 continued to live in camps in Thailand.[21]

In spite of great risks and high costs in human lives—especially for the boat refugees—the horrors of terrorism and deprivations were such that these people ventured to escape. An editorial in the French left-wing newspaper *Le Monde* ran as follows:

The tragedy which its people experience, is not caused by a foreign imperialist power but by the domestic imperialism of the ruling party.

If the Vietnamese people today cry out from hunger, it is not due to the willfulness of the climate but to an economic policy in which dogma has won over common sense. Dreadful terrorism is practiced against dissidents, a terrorism with slave camps and prisons—the Vietnamese Gulag.[22]

Retreat from Socialism

The consciousness of seeds of evil within us as possibilities functions as a barrier to all utopian projects aiming at eradication of evil from the society. When translated into political action they without exception lead to totalitarian tyranny.

Leszek Kolakowski, 1982

After the disastrous crop failures of 1977 and 1978, a harsh discussion was initiated between the hard-line socialist left wing and the more pragmatic right wing of Vietnam's Communist party. The discussion concerned economic policy and the need for stronger material incentives for the people working in production. This internal political struggle was won by the pragmatists. According to the party in a moment of self-criticism, sufficient attention had not been paid to the people's natural demand for material rewards. Even such political principles as equal pay and social equality had attenuated the will to work, and it was thought that hard work had to be made more profitable. A system with differentiated wages and piecework rates, already in effect in the South, was introduced in the North.

The most radical retreat from socialism has taken place in the Northern collective farms—in forms very similar to those undertaken in China. "Food is more important than principles"—so goes one of the pragmatic slogans of the party today, and land that formerly was held collectively has now been divided among the peasant families. Each family must deliver certain quantities to the collective—that is, to the state—and is paid according to prices set by the government. Any surplus the families can produce they may sell at more favorable prices on currently permitted free markets. Even if the peasants have not regained the formal rights of ownership of the land they cultivate, they have to some extent regained their status as free entrepreneurs, a change that ought to strengthen their incentives to work and produce. Recent large increases in procurement prices will work in the same direction.

In addition to these "capitalist" agrarian reforms, the anticapitalist offensive that was initiated in 1978 has been quietly dropped and has, in fact, been replaced by a diametrically opposite program. The roadblocks around Saigon that prevented peasants from transporting their surpluses to the city in order to sell them on black markets to the starving city dwellers have been removed, and the black markets have been converted into legal free markets. The most important source of food and other goods in Saigon now are 15,000 private street stands. Private trading, private service firms, and private manufacturing firms with a maximum of twenty employees not only are permitted, they are encouraged.

The "new economic policy" has clearly had favorable effects on production and supply, but the problems are far from solved. In 1982 Le Duan, secretary general of the party, admitted that mistakes had been made and that the latest five-year plan had not succeeded in correcting all of them. But he also employed the usual tactics of blaming the failures on scapegoats. This time a poor harvest could not be blamed solely on bad weather. Other villains were dredged up: "opportunists whose revolutionary fervor had abated, exploiters, smugglers, bullies, and corrupt people who took bribes."[23]

Chapter 12

Sri Lanka

> Sri Lanka offers perhaps the most extraordinary example of
> a nation with high food potential, yet with a serious food
> shortage. Farmers have simply been dissuaded from realiz-
> ing the land's potential.
>
> *Ronald C. Nairn,* American agrarian expert, 1979

From Granary to Shortage

> Every government that has tried to cut the rice ration has lost the
> upcoming election; every opposition promising larger food subsidies
> has assumed power.
>
> *C. A. Wachtmeister,* Swedish diplomat 1977

Sri Lanka is an island south of India with 15 million inhabitants, 600,000
of whom live in the capital city of Colombo. The country became
independent in 1948 and had since 1946 a constitution of parliamentary
democracy. Like most former colonial countries, Sri Lanka chose to
become a socialist welfare state. It eventually developed into an extraordinarily advanced welfare state, whose structure and economic situation
in 1977 was described by the German weekly *Die Welt:*

> Sri Lanka had [in 1977] developed to the most advanced welfare
> state outside of Scandinavia. Every citizen—whether poor or
> wealthy—received two free kilos of rice monthly from the state.

Bread, flour, sugar, and textiles were sold at extensively subsidized prices. Education from elementary school to university was free as were visits to doctors, hospital care, and lawyer consultations.

There was, however, a problem: The economy, socialized to 90 percent, was able to fulfill the welfare promises no more. Basic foodstuffs were certainly cheap, but could be bought only after hours of waiting in lines outside the stores—if they could be acquired at all. State subsidies consumed more than half of the national budget.[24]

Agriculture was not socialized, but, following the normal socialist pattern, the government set procurement prices for agricultural products far below the market level. As always, the aim was to favor the industrial and urban population, on whose support the regime based its power. The American agricultural expert Ronald C. Nairn says of this policy and its effects:

> To an appreciable degree, the Sri Lanka case is the story of thirty-eight countries where politicians have decreed price controls on food. It is nothing less than simple exploitation of farmers to subsidize ephemeral industrial development (which does not occur). More importantly, it allows politicians to buy and maintain power through the urban population—that is, the political part of the population.[25]

Exploitation of the peasants quickly killed their will to work to produce surpluses for sale. Many adapted to a subsistence agriculture, producing no more than their families needed. Soon this country, which had been more than self-supporting, had to import food and, finally, to import as much as a third of what it needed, an import consuming half of its export income.

The Collapse of the Welfare State

The state is that great fictitious entity by which everyone seeks to live at the expense of everyone else.

Frédéric Bastiat, 1846

Sirimavo Bandaranaike was prime minister of Sri Lanka for most of the years between 1960 and 1977—the first woman in modern times to hold such a position. Her political ambitions were focused on the building of a modern welfare state that would surpass comparable states in providing for the ordinary citizen. Following the model of the ancient Roman welfare state, she distributed rice, the national staple, free to the people. But a poor, underdeveloped country such as Sri Lanka cannot afford to pay for such handouts with its own resources; eventually, the "luxury consumption" had to be financed through foreign borrowing. But obtaining credits became more and more difficult; the growing debt meant a declining creditworthiness, and greater risks for the lenders meant higher interest rates and stricter amortization terms. The growing costs of debt service meant that the nation was obliged to seek new credits. The end of the credit road was at hand.

By the 1970s Sri Lanka had approached this critical third stage. Continuously shrinking flows of capital from abroad meant ever-increasing shortages of raw materials, fuels, semimanufactures, and spare parts for industry. Production was severely hampered, and a fourth of the labor force eventually lost their jobs. Sufficient funds for wages, subsidies, and other expenses could no longer be raised. The welfare system collapsed.

Accustomed to privileges of an extensive public welfare system, the people refused to face the reality of the situation. The electorate expressed its disappointment by voting for parties that promised to reestablish public welfare. At long last they were forced to learn their lessons, however, and acknowledge that fundamentally new policies were needed.

Sri Lanka is an outstanding example of a populist welfare state with a parliamentary democratic system—a country in which political parties have always tried to buy the political support of the electorate with generous promises of more welfare benefits and more subsidies—promises that could be fulfilled only by extensive loans.

Bandaranaike's Freedom Party, which was largely responsible for the foreign borrowing, tried to stay in power by promising ever more public welfare. After the final collapse of the welfare system, the emptiness of the party's promises became all too apparent, and in the 1977 election the opposing United National Party won a landslide victory on a platform that promised an end to socialist policy and welfare extravagance and an establishment of a market economy with incentives geared to efficient production.

Not only the domestic policies were changed radically. Under the leadership of Prime Minister—later President—Junius Jayewardene, the new regime began to lean toward the West and tried to win support there, especially in the United States. In 1981 Sri Lanka applied for membership in the Association of South East Asian Nations (ASEAN), an organization of five non-Communist countries—Indonesia, Malaysia, the Philippines, Singapore, and Thailand.

Must the Road to Renewal Pass through Collapse and Chaos?

We cannot depend on a government of any party to liquidate the welfare state as an act of patriotism or in response to public preferences. In the end it will be market forces that will make the welfare state yield to private choice and technical advance.

Arthur Seldon, British economist, 1981

Must a welfare state pursue its course to inevitable collapse? Is it not possible to perceive what is happening and to change the course of events in time? To anticipate the drying up of foreign sources of capital? To see the necessity of adapting public welfare programs to what the domestic economy can afford?

Experiences seem to confirm the dismal fact that to anticipate future threats and change the course in time to avoid troubles is extremely difficult in a parliamentary democracy. Any party that tires to prevent impending collapse through austerity programs is bound to meet with indignant protest and to lose elections. Each group considers its own interests sacrosanct; sacrifices simply must be made elsewhere. Proposed savings, then, generally mean "social disarmament," with severe consequences for groups that are socially weak—families with children, the sick, the unemployed, the aged.

In any welfare state the citizens, following well-established patterns of behavior, are always prepared to demand more welfare and to fiercely defend existing welfare benefits. The citizenry in such states, moreover, is organized into trade unions and associations, with shop stewards or other representatives who are paid and trained to claim more for their groups and to defend existing privileges with their last breath.

The collapse of the public welfare system of Sri Lanka could have been anticipated. But the majority of the citizens refused to take forecasts and warnings seriously. The political parties that proposed saving and a reduction of public welfare benefits were regularly defeated at the elections. Not until theory and projection had become fact, not until the entire welfare system had collapsed, not until shortages, lines, and deprivation had become the daily experience, not until manufacturers, for lack of materials, fuels, and other necessary inputs, had been forced to stop production and dismiss personnel, did the citizens realize that radically new policies were needed.

The new regime took over a society in ruin; it began reconstruction from scratch. It was not necessary to deprive people of public welfare benefits they had enjoyed earlier; that thankless task had been accomplished during the chaos and collapse of the previous government. The new government did not have to raise low, subsidized prices; state price-control and subsidy systems had collapsed under the previous government and prices had already risen explosively.

Since 1977, with the advent of the Jayewardene government, the people have seen positive results. No fewer than one million new jobs have been created, and unemployment has shrunk from 24 percent in 1977 to 10 percent in 1983. Food supply has increased decidedly, and the lines outside the stores have been eliminated. Production incentives have been restored in agriculture and in other industries, and the average annual growth rate since 1977 has been 6 percent. Welfare benefits had to be cut drastically by the new government, but in spite of severe withdrawal pains, the citizens were obliged to acknowledge that the new policies worked. Their confidence and satisfaction were demonstrated in 1979 and 1982, when the United National Party won the elections by a large margin.

In order to give the domestic economy a boost, private foreign enterprises, through state advertisements in Western papers and journals, were invited to invest and establish themselves in Sri Lanka; they were promised low taxes and free disposal of profits. Singapore was the model here. As in Singapore, Sri Lanka established a free zone, in which by

1983 some forty foreign enterprises with 20,000 employees had been installed.

Most of Sri Lanka's earlier high tariff walls have been pulled down. Rather than prevent imports, the new regime has tried to stimulate exports by creating a favorable entrepreneurial environment.

Chapter 13

Ghana

> The most urgent task of the social sciences ought to be studies concerning the unintended consequences of intended human action.
>
> *Karl Popper,* 1957

The Rapid Destruction of a Healthy Environment

> I fear we are headed for a period of permanent food crisis in Africa.
>
> *Maurice Williams,* executive director, World Food Council, 1981

During the colonial period, Ghana with its 12 million inhabitants—Accra, the largest city, has nearly a million—was called the Gold Coast, because gold had been discovered there. When in 1957 it became independent, Ghana was the first African country to have its native population assume power. Kwame Nkrumah, Ghana's president from 1960, was a great admirer of Soviet and Chinese Communism. Under the banner of "African socialism," he was determined to install a Communist system in his own country.

Cocoa was the dominant export commodity, and Ghana at its independence was by far the largest producer of cocoa in the world. According to the new regime, cocoa would be the milk cow to nourish rapid industrialization and an extensive welfare system, the two central features in the proposed program.

But it was the cocoa growers who would be milked. Low procurement prices were set by the state purchasing monopoly. They were set at such low levels that the government could reap fat profits when the cocoa was exported, and, as in feudal times, the great mass of peasants were left impoverished.

The peasants, of course, did their best to escape being robbed. They sold their surpluses on the black market, and those living near the border ventured to smuggle their crops to neighboring countries—primarily Togo and the Ivory Coast—at prices two or three times as high as government procurement prices in Ghana. Naturally, the peasants soon lost incentives to produce, and cocoa production, on which the socialist regime had planned to live well, only shriveled. Compare the development of production in the four most important cocoa-producing countries of the world:

TABLE 5

Production of Cocoa Beans from 1960 to 1982 (in thousands of tons)

Country	1960	1964	1970	1974	1978	1982
Brazil	160	154	197	181	309	314
Ivory Coast	94	145	179	185	350	456
Ghana	439	581	406	416	270	225
Nigeria	198	298	305	241	180	181

Source: United Nations, Food and Agricultural Organization: *Production Yearbook.*

From a modest start, Brazil and the Ivory Coast, two nonsocialist market states, have steadily increased their share of the market, and by 1977 both of them had caught up with and surpassed Ghana, hitherto the leading producer.

Ghana is a textbook case of a country in which the government, through price controls and a state purchasing monopoly, has demonstrated an ability to destroy the entrepreneurial environment rapidly. The consequences—for exports, imports, the standard of living, and economic growth—have been fatal.

The Art of Converting a Rich Country into a Poor One

I am afraid that within ten years Africa will be ruled everywhere by small poorly equipped armies which, nonetheless, will lord over the rest of the population.

Gunnar Myrdal, 1971

By now Ghana has passed through the typical life cycle of a socialist country. After most of its capital resources had dried up and the foreign credit potential had been consumed, sorely needed imports had to be cut drastically. Because of shortage and bottlenecks, only half of the country's production potential could be realized. The economy passed into the third stage of socialism: crisis. Domestic production could provide only half of the basic foods needed, such as maize, rice, and yams.

Cocoa production, which in 1964–1965 had amounted to 581,000 tons of beans, shrank eighteen years later, in 1982–1983, to less than 30 percent of its former volume—178,000 tons. This could only mean a catastrophic reduction in government revenues. In turn, the government became deficient in its maintenance of roads and bridges, and with an ensuing fuel crisis, communications and transportation collapsed entirely. Only half the 225,000 tons of cocoa beans purchased by the government in 1980–1981 could be transported to the coastal ports and exported. The rest was left to rot.

The Ghanaian economy was quickly proclaimed Africa's most chaotic—a title won in hard competition with other candidates. The country's economic situation in early 1983 was described by an American journalist:

> Many factories have closed completely for lack of materials, while those that remain open commonly operate at only 10 percent of capacity. Harvests of cassava, the staple vegetable of the Ghanaian diet, have fallen to 1.8 million tons, down from 3.6 million tons ten years ago.

Ghana's greatest single economic failure, however, has been the precipitous drop in cocoa production, which accounts for 70% of the country's exports. Only 200,000 tons will be produced this year, in contrast to 500,000 tons twelve years ago. The reason: successive regimes forced artificially low prices on farmers, who then abandoned cocoa for more lucrative crops. Meantime, the country's already dwindling export earnings were poured into industrial projects that have largely failed. As a result, Ghana's foreign debt exceeds $2 billion, the equivalent of two years' exports.[26]

The government found various scapegoats—increased oil prices, poor weather, and so on—but the real cause of the crisis was clearly government policy. One of the most popular scapegoats among developing countries—lack of natural resources—could not be used by Ghana. It is one of the world's best endowed countries: Fertile soil, ample rainfall, and a favorable climate create an ideal natural environment for agriculture. Several crops a year can usually be harvested. There are also rich finds of manganese, bauxite, oil, diamonds, and gold. As a producer of gold, Ghana occupied fifth place among the countries of the world in 1974, a position it could not maintain; by 1981 it had fallen to ninth place.

Price control is an essential part of government policy in Ghana; state regulation is applied *as if* the objective were to destroy industry and curtail production. Seldom in history has the eradication of market prices cost so much in political prices as in Ghana.

Pegged exchange rates, in particular, have had devastating consequences for foreign trade in Ghana. In 1978 the rate for the cedi, the Ghanaian monetary unit, was set by the government at 2.75 cedi to the dollar; while the rate on the black market was 40. The sellers in black markets operate at extreme risk and must include risk premiums in their prices. These premiums, in the form of extremely high prices, are paid by consumers who are unable to acquire food and other necessities on the legal markets.

If it is assumed that the exchange rate for the cedi on a legal free market would have been 27.50—40 minus a risk premium of 12.50—it must be concluded that in 1978 exporters were deprived of 90 percent of their capital. When exchanging their earned dollars, they should have received 27.50 cedis per dollar, but they actually received only 2.75. Nobody can afford to export on such terms—in effect a 90 percent tax on export commodities. All Ghanaian exporters in 1978 had to circumvent the state regulations, whether legally or illegally. The government of Ghana, moreover, had set such low prices on fifteen "vital" commodities that all production of these commodities and legal trade in them had become impossible. Only because the black markets took over production and distribution entirely was disaster prevented.

But production incentives were seriously weakened by price controls. Those consumers whom the government wanted to favor by instituting price controls actually paid more and were able to buy less than they would have in a free market with free prices. Once more the observer is reminded of the *Mises effect*, expressed in Ludwig von Mises' own words:

> Economics does not say that isolated government interference with the prices of only one commodity or a few commodities is unfair, bad, or unfeasible. It says that such interference produces results contrary to its purpose, that it makes conditions worse, not better, from the point of view of the government and those backing its interference.[27]

The International Monetary Fund, Ghana's principal source of foreign credit, has done its best to make the country's economic policies more rational. The IMF was willing to grant further credits only if the following conditions were fulfilled:

- A radical devaluation of the currency.
- A radical increase in the procurement price of cocoa.
- A radical increase in fuel prices.

In November 1981 the procurement price of cocoa was raised from 120 cedi to 360 cedi for a 30-kilo sack, thereby seemingly fulfilling the second condition—but only seemingly. The tripling of the price was obviously insufficient to compensate for inflation, the rate of which was approximately 100 percent a year.

For several reasons, the government was less willing to accede to the first condition, devaluation. Such a measure would mean an explosion of the prices of imported commodities, something that would be disliked intensely by the urban population, the political supporters of the government. Although the low, controlled prices made imports impossible, people seemed to prefer low nominal prices and do without the imported commodities rather than pay higher prices and have such commodities available.

Under pressure to devalue, moreover, all governments see their currency as a national symbol, a banner. Devaluation is not only an official admission of political failure but also a national humiliation, comparable to striking the colors. Even though radical devaluation is an absolute requisite for a revitalization of legal exports, a weak government will postpone it as long as possible.

Similar shortsightedness has prevented the government from raising the price of motor fuels. The low price level at which fuels are now set stimulates luxury consumption among the privileged city dwellers with private cars, as well as preventing imports. The lack of fuel has contributed to Ghana's transportation and communication collapse. By 1984, to make matters worse, electricity was available only every second day.

The Ghanaian situation aptly illustrates the devastating consequences of setting prices politically rather than letting the market determine them in a country in which a weak government, dependent on the goodwill of consumer groups, does not dare to prescribe price increases that are absolutely necessary. The problem of politically controlled prices is to be found not only in all socialist welfare states but in many capitalist welfare states as well. Seldom, if ever, was a low price policy driven to such absurd extremes as in Ghana, however. And seldom, if ever, has a rich country been transformed into a poor one as rapidly and unequivocally as has Ghana.

The Political Father of Ghana

> The control of the production of wealth is the control of human life itself.
>
> *Hilaire Belloc,* 1912

The fact that the first political leader of Ghana, Kwame Nkrumah, prime minister from 1957 and president from 1960, originally was something of a father figure who enjoyed great prestige within and outside the country, does not mitigate the devastating effects on industry and on the provision of goods that were the logical and inevitable consequences of his socialist policies. Dissatisfaction among Nkrumah's hard-hit subjects grew to such proportions that in 1966—less than a decade after the achievement of national independence—the military leaders considered it their duty to interfere and depose Nkrumah. Although the military junta eventually entrusted power to civil governments, the new governments remained dependent on the favor and support of the military forces. Although each new government began with solemn vows to abolish inflation, corruption, stagnation, and shortages, conditions grew steadily worse, and after a short time the government had exhausted the nation's goodwill and had to resign. Nor did the situation improve when Air Force Lieutenant Jerry Rawlings assumed power in a military coup in 1979 or when, after a civilian interlude, he again seized power on New Year's Eve in 1981.

Ghana was the first of the old colonial areas in Africa to become an independent nation, and it is understandable that the population as well as the political leaders lived in ecstasy over their independence, trusting that national freedom and socialism together would be the keys to the door of a happy and prosperous future. It is equally understandable that in the independence year of 1957 Kwame Nkrumah, as the new nation's first political leader, would make the following vow:

> It is Ghana's duty to prove that Africans can rule themselves and also prove that they, in a democratic system, can be both efficient and tolerant. Ghana must take the lead and function as a model for all of Africa.[28]

Nkrumah lived in exile from 1966 until his death in 1972. On March 6, 1982, when Ghana celebrated its twenty-fifth anniversary as a free nation, no one was indiscreet enough to bring up Nkrumah's vow.

When close to one million refugees of Ghanaian origin were expelled from Nigeria in early 1983 and were forced to return to their homeland, the economic and social situation in Ghana was, of course, under greater strain than ever.

Chapter 14

Tanzania

> If we had just wished to be happy. To achieve happiness would have been easy. But we wish to be more happy than others, which is difficult, because we believe others to be happier than they actually are.
>
> *Charles de Montesquieu, 1748*

Socialization Policies After 1961

> Those who promised us paradise on earth never produced anything but a hell.
>
> *Karl Popper, 1945*

Tanzania, with a population of 19 million in 1983, of whom 900,000 lived in the capital city of Dar es Salaam, became an independent nation in 1961. Julius Nyerere, a confirmed socialist, was elected president in 1962.

During its early years, the government was fully occupied with the transformation of the country from a colonial area under British hegemony to a free nation. In 1967, however, the so-called Arusha Declaration, a program for the implementation of socialism in the economy, was issued. Subsequently, all important industrial enterprises, including banks, insurance companies, export trade companies, and even many of the larger plantations, were socialized.

In Tanzania 90 percent of the population had earned their livelihood as small peasants in scattered settlements. According to the Soviet model, such a multitude of small, "inefficient" farms had to be concentrated into large "efficient" collectives—called *ujamaa* villages. The program to socialize agriculture was sketched out only roughly in the Arusha Declaration. Some months later in 1967, President Nyerere issued the publication *Socialism and Rural Development*, in which he presented the detailed program. Among the principles that were to govern the transformation Nyerere listed:

- Respect for the individual.
- Compulsory work.
- Cooperative enterprises.
- Voluntary migration into the collectives.

And according to the socialization plan, the transformation was to take place in three stages:

- After families had been resettled in large villages, the land was temporarily to be cultivated privately.
- The transition into collective production was to be effected gradually and quietly.
- The ultimate stage, a collective large-scale agriculture, was to be achieved by persuasion, not by force. Private plots were to be allowed.

Although the peasants were tantalized with schools, shops, centers for medical care, and drilled wells in the *ujamaa* villages, the voluntary resettlement for which the government had hoped made only slow progress. In order to speed up migration, the government made further offers: free transportation to the collectives, free building materials, free food until the first crop was harvested, free agricultural machinery, and access to credit on favorable terms. But in spite of the government's increased generosity and intensified propaganda campaigns, the peasants were reluctant; by 1974 only 2.5 million people had moved into the collectives.

The government now had to choose between accepting a situation in which only 20 percent of the program had been carried out or giving up the principle of voluntarism. The government chose the latter and applied such strict and effective methods that during the two subsequent years the population in the *ujamaa* villages increased from 2.5 million to 13 million. With 90 percent of the peasants concentrated in the collectives, the plan was nearly fulfilled. In order to prevent peasants from stealing back to their homes, the government often had the old settlements burned.

The Collapse of Collectivism

Men in power, using the law as an instrument of plunder, are the worst of social evils, as they erase from everyone's conscience the distinction between right and wrong, and so undermine that respect for law without which no society can exist.

Frédéric Bastiat, 1846

The harsh, sometimes brutal treatment of the rural population proved that the socialists who had assumed power in Tanzania, despite all the humane principles they endorsed, were no different from their counterparts in other socialist countries. In the effort to socialize they did not hesitate to employ force. Even in a country as rurally oriented as Tanzania, the rural population became the outgroup—tools for the achievement of a socialist goal.

According to the plans, each *ujamaa* village was to be settled by an average of 250 families, and these families, using modern technology and machines, were to cultivate the vast land areas belonging to the village. The plans were only socialist dreams, however, and never amounted to more than that. Today perhaps a dozen of the 8,000 *ujamaa* villages function more or less in accordance with the original plan. In the others, most of the land has been divided up, and each family now cultivates its own fields as if they were private property.

This retreat from socialist agriculture is in many ways similar to corresponding retreats in China and Vietnam. It does not, however, imply a return to the original system, in which peasants cultivated small, scattered private settlements. At great disadvantage to private farming, the peasants still live in the new large villages. The distance from the village to each family's field is now greater than it was before the concentration of the settlement, and the women must walk long distances to gather the dry wood that is needed as fuel for cooking.

The Oppression of the Peasantry

> The agencies in Tanzania which, acting as State monopolies, set prices and trade with agricultural commodities have grown into unwieldy, inefficient, and expensive bureaucracies—parasites on the rural population. Sweden bears a responsibility for this policy, which it not only supported but honored as progressive.
>
> *Carl Hamilton,* Swedish Social-Democratic economist, 1982

The ruthlessness of Tanzanians in power was bound to produce distrust and bitterness among the peasants, and these feelings only served to dampen their will to work. When the government bludgeoned them further by instituting price controls on agricultural products, the majority of the peasants began to produce only enough for their own needs. Like the Ghanaians, what surpluses the Tanzanian peasants had they sold on the black markets. As always under such circumstances, consumers had to pay exorbitant prices, including the standard black-market premium to compensate the sellers for the risks of punishment. Peasants living near the borders would smuggle their surpluses into neighboring countries, where prices were usually many times higher than the controlled domestic prices. In its efforts to stop the smuggling, the Tanzanian government in 1977 closed the border to Kenya (it was reopened in November 1983). The price Tanzania had to pay was the loss of a profitable tourist trade and the loss of income from the considerable transit traffic between Kenya and Zambia.

Tanzanian leaders, like their brothers in other socialist countries, have always maintained that their chief objective is to help the poor and weak in their society; it was this message that was given special emphasis in Tanzania's Arusha Declaration. In reality, the socialists have pursued an opposite policy, favoring the prosperous and the strong—the industrial workers, the police, the soldiers, the bureaucracy—and plundering the weakest members of the population, the peasants. The gap between theory and practice, rhetoric and reality, in this "model country" has been wide indeed.

Growth in Tanzania will not come about unless the entrepreneurs— the peasants—are given a social and economic environment with strong production incentives. And until Tanzania can proceed from socialistic rhetoric to the realistic institution of measures that involve its people, the economic crisis of Tanzania can only worsen.

Stagnation and Shortages

> Poverty is no more the major obstacle to development in the social- ist countries of the third world. It is socialism itself. Tanzania is a nation in a state of decay. The socialist experiment has brought them chaos, corruption, inefficiency and crime.
>
> *Svenska Dagbladet,* February 9, 1981

By 1979, five years after the enforced resettlement, domestic agricultural production in Tanzania was already incapable of providing the cities with food. Imports had to be increased to compensate for declining production, and in 1980 no less than half of the food needed by Tanzania was being imported. A decade of socialist agricultural policy had been sufficient to destroy the socio-ecological system. In a fundamentally agricultural economy in which 80 percent of the export income in the past had come from agricultural surpluses, a growing share of the dwin- dling export income in recent years had had to be used to pay for imports of food.

So far it has been possible to finance large imports through foreign aid programs and by borrowing from abroad, but the intensifying eco- nomic crisis has made potential lenders less and less willing. Shortages of necessary materials have followed, and, as a consequence, the volume of industrial production in 1982 was reduced by half. A report in a Norwegian newspaper stated:

> Large sectors of the production system stand still, food lines in the capital city of Dar es Salaam were never longer, and shop shelves never more empty.[29]

Shortages of fuels and spare parts, and a general lack of maintenance of the roads, caused the whole communication system to collapse. The lack of transport facilities meant among other things that food surpluses produced in different regions often were left to rot. The peasants were thus not inclined to produce surpluses. Even electricity production and telephone communications were hit hard—they functioned only intermittently.

Tanzania started a national airline, an important status symbol among developing countries, but by 1981 Air Tanzania was forced to take two newly purchased planes out of circulation because of a shortage of spare parts, and traffic to countries abroad had to be canceled.

Every year since 1979, according to official declarations, Tanzania has suffered crop failures because of drought, heavy rains, or floods. Long experience dictates that agricultural policies and bad weather are bound to be eternal companions.

Foreign Aid

Should we really lengthen the death agonies of socialist experiments in countries whose intellectual power groups are dependent on capital supply from the Western world?

F. A. Hayek, 1974

As the Soviet Union and, later, Cuba proved more and more unfit to serve as models for the socialists of the Western world, Tanzania after the Arusha Declaration in 1967 began to take their place. There, it was thought, the dreams would be realized. For tactical reasons, the word socialism was seldom mentioned in Tanzania. Those in power preferred to talk about "cooperation," a concept with a positive timbre, even among nonsocialists. Tanzania was touted as a model of socialist development policy. It is thus not surprising that Tanzania became the pet child of Western aid to developing countries during the six years between 1976 and 1982.

That the political leaders of Tanzania, like their counterparts in Vietnam and Cuba, have squandered a great deal of their scanty resources for military adventures in neighboring countries has been difficult for world opinion to digest. The war against the Idi Amin regime in Uganda during 1979 to 1982 was unreasonably expensive for Tanzania.

The Arusha Declaration stated that the fundamental economic goal was to develop the Tanzanian economy in such a way that it would become self-supporting, independent of foreign aid. The truth is, however, that the country was never farther from being self-supporting or independent of foreign aid than during recent years. In 1982, a journalist reported:

> Roughly 70 percent of all products have been financed with foreign money. . . . Only small amounts of foreign currencies are left in the Tanzanian exchequer, most communications are at a standstill, and of the industrial potential only 60 percent is utilized.[30]

The dismal reality is emerging, and the lenders and deliverers of foreign aid are beginning to express doubts about Tanzania. The flow of resources from abroad has been curtailed considerably during recent years and threatens to, dry up entirely.

The Last Days of the Nyerere Regime

> You, the people of our country, have laid upon me a heavy burden of responsibility. This burden I have accepted with a sense of humility and of gratitude.
>
> *Julius Nyerere,* in his inaugural address, 1962

After a visit to Tanzania in 1982, a Norwegian radio commentator delivered the following picture of a country in deep economic decay:

> On days when bread was delivered to the stores, people had to line up for hours. Even commodities like soap, toothpaste, salt, flour, cooking oil, batteries and bandages were lacking. People starve, and starving people get desperate. When I visited Tanzania in 1974 many things were lacking, too, but the people still had optimism

and enthusiasm. They listened to President Nyerere: if they worked harder, the future would be better. Now the President's calls have lost their magic; people are resigned. The brutal truth is that the policy of President Nyerere has completely failed. . . . The Tanzanians are unable to manage the many state enterprises, and today production is only 30 percent of its volume a few years ago.[31]

Responsibility for economic and social developments during a government's reign must be borne by that government. For the Nyerere government, the burden was too heavy to bear, and it desperately tried to find convenient scapegoats. On April 5, 1983, President Nyerere in a long and emotional speech declared war against corruption and black-market speculators. He urged the people to report all persons selling commodities on black markets. Offenders were not to be judged by ordinary courts but sent directly to the countryside to work in agriculture. The country could not afford the juridical "shows" at the courts. One week after the speech at least four hundred civil servants, businessmen, and black-market "speculators" were arrested.

The president never mentioned that corruption and black markets were natural results of shortages created by Tanzanian government policies. Nor did he mention that high black-market prices had in fact stimulated production of food and other necessities which otherwise would never have been provided and thereby actually saved countless Tanzanian lives. Nor did he mention that his campaign against black markets would worsen the shortages and mean starvation and death for many.

Aware of the severe economic and social crisis at hand, the army leaders decided to interfere. Twenty Tanzanian officers tried to overthrow the Nyerere regime in January 1983; it was a coup that failed. More and more Tanzanians would agree that an army revolt may be their only possible salvation from an unbearable situation. When will the next one come?

Chapter 15

Cuba

> Poor Cuban people—emerging from the Batista plague to be inflicted by the Castro cholera.
>
> *Fernando Arrabal,* Spanish author in exile, 1982

The Shangri-La of Socialism

> What has always made the state a hell on earth has been precisely that man has tried to make it his heaven.
>
> *Friedrich Hoelderlin,* 1797

In Cuba, which now has a population of 10 million, 1 million of whom live in the capital city of Havana, a socialist group under the leadership of Fidel Castro seized power in January 1959. Ideologically, the group was closely allied to the Soviet Union, which in subsequent years gave the new socialist state comprehensive economic support.

All landed estates of more than 400 hectares of cropland were socialized—that is, confiscated—in May of 1959. Most of them were foreign-owned sugar and tobacco plantations. A further step on the road to socialism was taken in 1963 when estates of more than 67 hectares were socialized.

No collective farms were included in the plans—a deviation from the Soviet model. Most of the large confiscated estates and plantations were converted into state farms, while a small part of the land was distributed to agricultural workers as small farms. Since all the land was socialized, the many private peasants became tenants. They were, however, exempted from payment of both rent and taxes, so the land reform enjoyed great popularity, at least in the initial stage. Later, enthusiasm was dampened significantly by price controls, which meant low payments to the peasants for their products. All industry, trade, and transportation enterprises except small family firms were also socialized, as were all rented dwellings.

The new regime was extraordinarily "generous" in its policy. Not only were private peasants exempted from paying rent and taxes, tenants in rented dwellings, too, were exempted from paying rent. Passengers in public transportation facilities did not have to pay, and no charge was made for calls from telephone booths. Education and health care were free. In the general socialist enthusiasm, no one asked where the government of this impoverished land would find resources to pay for this cavalier generosity. The new regime obviously wanted to conceive a socialist Shangri-La, where all needs would be satisfied, free of charge.

Socialism and Shortages: Unescapable Companions

People in the West do not comprehend the misery that is in Cuba. There are just two categories of people: wardens and prisoners.

Cosme Caballero, Cuban refugee of 1980

The new socialist regime, which had confiscated all land and all enterprises without compensating the former owners, the "capitalists," seemed to have all the advantages on its side. While the earlier capitalist enterprises had been burdened by large debt-service payments, by rents and leases, the socialist enterprises could start from scratch, entirely free of such burdens. Such a situation must seem to a capitalist businessman like a dream of paradise. Certainly, to all the world's socialist dreamers, it looked like a paradise. Quite soon, however, it would become apparent that most of all it resembled a fool's paradise.

To confiscate the production apparatus of a country with arms and violence—the earlier owners called it robbery—was a simple operation for the victors of the revolution. A decidedly more difficult operation would be to make the apparatus function productively under the new conditions of a socialist system.

In Cuba this task was made even more difficult by the fact that Castro and his colleagues, like typical socialist dreamers, believed that people would work hard, fired with enthusiasm for the holy cause of socialism without the incentive of normal wages and payments. In Cuba the realities surfaced quickly and indisputably. Both agriculture and industry functioned poorly in the new socialist system, a fact that was mercilessly exposed by shortages of food and necessities—shortages that meant bitter hardship. Employing an extensive system of rationing, the political leaders tried to distribute scarce supplies in a socially acceptable manner. People were made to believe that shortages and lines were infant maladies of socialism, temporary annoyances that would soon disappear. They did not disappear, however, and the rationing system not only continued but expanded.

Forced Labor and Militarization

The revolutionary enthusiasm that the workers displayed during the initial period soon began to cool. Low wages and the meager supplies of life's necessities apportioned to them diminished their will to work, and absenteeism in state enterprises increased rapidly until it amounted to a third of the labor force.

When a socialist regime is forced to admit that socialist enthusiasm is not sufficient incentive to inspire energetic work, it occasionally learns its lessons and concludes that better material incentives are needed. Although Castro, in his many and lengthy speeches, occasionally hinted at such conclusions, most often he resorted to socialism's favorite remedy, coercion by the state.

Laws were passed against "loafing"—against "drones and parasites." The laws authorized the regime to control the work of all citizens by means of compulsory individual work books, and severe punishments for absenteeism were prescribed. Military forces were mobilized to function as inspectors and controllers of work performance, and they were ordered to take action against all truants. Often, especially during the harvest, the population was mobilized for so-called voluntary work, and even here soldiers were used to see that the people showed up for work and did what was expected of them.

Cuba is one of the world's largest producers of sugar, which is its dominant export crop. At an early stage the new regime declared that too strong an emphasis on sugar production—a kind of monoculture— was a form of capitalistic exploitation. Sugar was therefore to be replaced in part by other crops. In 1964, however, a sudden and complete reversal of policy was decided upon. The production of 10 million tons of sugar in 1970 was proclaimed as a new national goal. Since 7.2 million tons had been harvested twelve years earlier, the proclaimed goal should have been attainable. According to the plan, such an extensive supply of machines was to be available in 1970 that the greater part of the work of harvesting could be accomplished mechanically.

The plan proved to have been based on wishful thinking, for no more machines were available in 1970 than in 1964, and 98 percent of the sugar crop had to be harvested manually. In a desperate effort to fulfill the goal, the whole country was mobilized; more than a million "volunteers" were required. The mobilization was accomplished by means of persuasion, pressure, and threats, all supervised by military force. It was, in fact, forced labor. In spite of the "total mobilization of the people," no more than 8.5 million tons were produced—a new record, to be sure, but far from the proclaimed goal.

The extreme concentration of resources on the sugar sector had to be paid for with corresponding reductions in other sectors. The Castro regime had undoubtedly overstrained the forces at their disposal; for the next five years only an average of 5.6 million tons of sugar was produced annually. The 1970 record still held in 1983.

Economic Deterioration

> The water distribution board decided that water should be provided free of charge. . . . But what was the outcome? Water waste was incredible. Many did not bother to close the tap. People seemed oblivious of the need to economize water. The communist principle produced waste in the water supply.

> *Fidel Castro,* 1973

The inability of the regime to acquire machines for the sugar harvest in 1970 was typical. It simply was never able to afford such purchases. When a regime, according to the old Roman populist model, wants to buy the goodwill and support of the people by offering them such benefits as free education, free medical care, free or cheap communication facilities, housing, water, electricity, telephones, and price-controlled and subsidized food, the inevitable result is shortages in all these services and commodities, including a shortage of capital for investment and industrial development. Even worse, there will be a shortage of capital for reinvestment—that is, for repair and maintenance of existing assets.

If citizens are invited to live in existing dwellings and no rents are charged, there will be no capital available to maintain what is there nor to build new. A severe shortage of housing space will develop, and the existing stock of dwellings will deteriorate into slums. And if the citizens are offered free water, the waterworks and water mains will soon collapse for lack of maintenance. It is the same with electricity and communication facilities.

Similarly, there will not be sufficient capital to pay for free education and free medical care, and as a consequence standards will decline.

In industry, Cuban workers had to manage as long as possible with the old machines and tools. Because they lacked spare parts for maintenance and repair, and lacked capital for raw materials, fuels, and new machines, less and less of the equipment was usable, and production declined. The regime tried to assuage the situation by favoring the industrial workers and urban dwellers with cheap food. They did so by imposing price controls—once again at the expense of the peasants. But cheap food for the privileged only brought on shortages and ever longer lines. Eventually it became necessary to legalize the mushrooming black markets and to permit the peasants to sell their surpluses at free prices, a surrender to market forces similar to those in China and Vietnam.

In Cuba, as we have learned by now to expect, the poor harvests and food shortages were blamed on bad weather. Or on a fungus that caused an extremely poor tobacco crop in 1980, when Cuba, for the first time in its history, had to import tobacco. A socialist regime in command of the state coercion apparatus will have an easy enough time inventing a shortage of tobacco in Havana—or, for that matter, a paucity of coal in Newcastle.

The Right to Work

> I refuse to talk about Cuba in the same breath as about Pinochet's Chile, Somoza's Nicaragua, and Stroessner's Paraguay. But human rights must be defended wherever they are violated.
>
> *Per Wästberg,* Swedish author, 1979

The right to work is one of the rights granted legally to Cubans after the revolution of 1959. Before 1959 unemployment was high, and in 1962 8 percent of the labor force were reported to be still without jobs. Various methods of reducing unemployment were tried; one entailed doubling or tripling the number of workers on state farms and factories. Eventually full employment was achieved, and in 1978 complaints about a labor shortage were heard in Cuba, complaints that gave socialists in the unemployment-plagued West opportunities to speak proudly about the innate superiority of socialism.

In 1980, however, Castro was forced to admit that unemployment plagued Cuba once more. In the tobacco factories, where it had become necessary to lay off some 10,000 workers, the adverse situation could be blamed on a natural catastrophe, on the poor crop. In the building industry, where construction projects under way had to be stopped because of a shortage of building materials, acceptable explanations were more difficult to find. Many of the construction workers lost their jobs. The production of both cement and bricks required large volumes of oil, and Cuba could no longer afford to import as much oil as it had earlier.

Lacking capital to pay for imports, Cuba began to experience shortages, so production in the state enterprises declined. Despite the fact that significantly more workers than the situation warranted were retained, large numbers of people had to be laid off.

The new regime in Cuba had found it easy enough to enact a law granting everyone the right to work; far more difficult was the task of creating an economic and social environment in which the demand for labor would equal or surpass the supply—that is, an economy with full employment.

The Shrinking Flow of Aid

Economic support by the Soviet Union has been very important to Cuba. It regularly purchases half the Cuban sugar crop at a high price and delivers large quantities of oil to Cuba at a low price. Scores of technical and military experts and advisers have been sent to Cuba, along with extensive shipments of arms and war materiel. Many of the Soviet deliveries were out-and-out gifts, others were made possible by generous credits.

In recent years, however, the Soviet Union has found it increasingly difficult to dispense its resources so cavalierly. Four years of crop failures, falling prices for export staple commodities such as oil, natural gas, gold, and diamonds, and the acute needs of countries within the Soviet bloc, primarily Poland, for assistance have drastically reduced the Soviet Union's ability to offer aid. During recent years, Soviet aid to Cuba, therefore, has been gradually reduced in value and volume; Cuba's lack of fuel for the production of building materials is only one indicator of the wane of Soviet aid.

Not only has aid from the Soviet Union been reduced, but as Cuban socialism was revealed for its oppression and failures, the flow of foreign aid from other wealthy countries decreased significantly. And for Cuba, which has based its production as well as its public welfare service on extensive imports, foreign loans, and aid, such a substantial reduction of revenue is producing disastrous effects.

Flight from Paradise

> The primary right of man is to be allowed to live in freedom at home,
> not to be allowed to leave his native country for freedom abroad.
>
> *Ludvik Vaculik,* Czech author, 1982

Under no other government in its history has Cuba had as many exiles,
as many executed, and as many political prisoners as it has had under
the Castro government. The Cuban people cannot express criticism or
disappointment openly or through general free elections. Cubans, however, unlike many others in socialist countries, occasionally have been
allowed to vote with their feet. Between 1959 and 1971 some 250,000
Cubans were permitted to leave the country. The majority took the
quickest way—to Florida and the United States. But by 1971 the drain
was excessive and emigration was stopped.

In April 1980 the Cuban guard at the gates of the Peruvian embassy
in Havana was withdrawn, and thousands of Cubans saw their chance;
they took refuge on embassy grounds. After some difficult days of
uncertainty and privation, they were permitted to leave Cuba. The
national gates were, in fact, opened once more, and for five months a
stream of Cuban "boat refugees" was allowed to leave.

Since 1959 approximately 1 million Cubans—10 percent of the population—have left, demonstrating that they prefer life as refugees in a
foreign country to life as citizens of a socialist homeland.

A tree pulled up by the roots does not—according to Rabindranath
Tagore—thereby win its freedom. Every human being is deeply rooted
in his native land, and only severe hardship or threats of terror can make
10 percent of a country's population choose the life of a refugee.

Socialism's Promised Land—Dream and Reality

> The Swedes should not make themselves accomplices to a dictator-
> ship restricting liberty. Our sensibility to oppression must not be
> selective. We must not be indignant solely against crimes that have
> been committed or are being committed by dictatorships to the right.
>
> *Armando Valladares,* Cuban author in exile, 1983

By the early 1960s the socialist dreamers of the world had come to
realize—even to admit openly—that their hope for paradise, the Soviet

Union, had bitterly failed to fulfill their expectations. To these "homeless" dreamers, who had a strong need to anchor their hopes in a thriving socialist state, the Cuban Revolution of 1959 came as a welcome gift. The socialist pilgrims who had earlier thronged to socialism's first home, the Soviet Union, now found in Cuba a new ideological haven.

And for the socialists, Cuba seemed a model indeed—a country that offered not only free education and free health-care services found in capitalist welfare states, but free (or very inexpensive) water, electricity, land, housing, and communication facilities. The dream of Shangri-La, a dream as old as it is naive, had at last been realized in Cuba.

Since 1975 the reality behind the facade of Cuban socialism has been revealed. Socialism's idealists have had their eyes opened and have even admitted Cuba's failures. One journalist, as late as the fall of 1979, wrote in praise:

> Under Castro, Cuba has been and remains a model for the Third World. Free education, health care, and social welfare have become a reality for the majority.[32]

But appended to this homage, this dutiful declaration of fidelity to old ideas, was an observation of a number of regrettable "changes for the worse":

> The secret police have been given ever increasing powers and bureaucratization has become more and more similar to that described by Kafka. Authors are prevented from writing. Cuba's PEN club [an international association of authors] has long been inoperative. For many years the number of political prisoners has been the highest in the world. One out of every ten Cubans has left the country since the revolution.[32]

Chapter 16

Argentina

> Perón is the child of our mistakes. For decades we had the
> chance to do something about the great mass of poor people
> in both city and country and we missed that chance. Then
> Perón came along, saw the chance, and took it.
>
> *Russell H. Fitzgibbon,* 1952

Colonel Juan Perón

> In the book *The Hour of the People* Juan Perón anticipated social-
> ism's final victory in Latin America. He obviously considered himself
> a socialist, but never concealed his admiration for Mussolini.
>
> *Sixten Palm,* Swedish journalist, 1982

The seizure of power by a military junta in Argentina in June 1943 came
as a result of strong tensions over domestic policy between opposing
groups. One officer of that military group, Colonel Juan Perón, went
from virtual anonymity to absolute power. By December 1943 he was
made minister of labor; the following year he became minister of defense, and then vice-president. Perón soon became the leading political
personality, although many—including members of the military—
strongly criticized his "friend of the workers" image and "socialist"

policies. On several occasions during the autumn of 1945 various military groups tried to depose him, and by October of that year, one of the coups succeeded, and Perón was placed under arrest. But the workers and the powerful trade unions, for whom Perón was a champion, organized violent demonstrations in Buenos Aires, and forced Perón's adversaries to retreat. Perón was reinstated, his prestige vastly enhanced.

In February 1945 Perón was elected president of Argentina by an overwhelming majority—299 electoral votes out of 365. His principal supporters were the country's 7 million workers, including the agricultural workers—the "shirtless ones." *His* party, originally the Workers Party, was later renamed the Peronist Party. He never described himself as a socialist during that first period in power—a period that lasted until 1955—and the middle class supported him. During his subsequent years of exile in Spain, Perón evidently felt free to speak more openly.

Under the Banners of Socialism

I consider myself a socialist and feel deeply disappointed that the Soviets in power never realized this and so never supported me. My dream was, in fact, to become Argentina's Fidel Castro.

Juan Perón, in exile, 1965

A study of the economic policy pursued by Perón from 1943 to 1955 reveals great similarities to those we have come to recognize in the foregoing analyses of socialist states. Perón became president in June 1946, and within months presented a five-year plan, the primary focus of which (following the established socialist pattern) was the rapid industrialization of the country. The plan was strongly supported by the industrial workers, a privileged group under the Perón regime, who were granted cheap food, a shorter work week, vacations, a minimum wage, and the privilege to demand higher pay.

Many large companies in Argentina were foreign-owned. Because of poverty and lack of domestic investment capital, businessmen from abroad had been invited to build their enterprises in Argentina. But

Perón could not, either as a nationalist or as a socialist, accept this foreign "capitalism." His socialization—"nationalization"—of the railways, the telephone service, and many of the largest companies including banks and insurance companies, proved very popular with the masses.

The Argentine state industries, however, were inefficiently managed, and found it difficult to meet import competition from abroad. As a nationalist, Perón hastened to increase duties on imports in order to protect domestic industries; he applied this support so generously that duties on many commodities became prohibitive.

If rapid industrialization was the primary goal of the five-year plan, rapid expansion of the public welfare system was a clear second. The major part of the system was to be financed by a payroll tax to be paid by the employers. After a series of increases these taxes eventually amounted to 60 percent of the total wage budget.

Agricultural Policy and Its Consequences

> Perón bought agricultural products on the cheap and sold them dear to a hungry world. He regarded the farmlands as a milk cow with unfailing udders, but sooner or later the fount of plenty was bound to dry up.
>
> *Jack Winocur,* American journalist, 1952

The Argentine pampas comprise 500,000 square kilometers. A favorable climate and rich soil make the pampas one of the world's four most important agricultural areas, the others being southern Russia, northern China, and the prairies of North America. The per-capita area of the Argentine croplands today is 1.25 hectares; in the United States it is 0.83, in the Soviet Union, 0.87.[33]

But not even the best natural conditions can guarantee a food supply sufficient to feed a nation's population if the economic policies of the government will not encourage the farmers. Argentina under Perón managed to convert its surpluses into deficits.

The process follows the pattern of a textbook case. Perón, like his-socialist counterparts in other countries, based his power on the political support of the urban population, the industrial workers. For their loyalty, the city dwellers demanded cheap food, a favor they expected Perón to grant them by imposing state regulations. He met their demands with price controls, and by requiring the peasants to make compulsory deliveries to the state purchasing agency. From the beginning, procurement prices were set so low that the agency was able to export grain at a profit of 300 percent.

In his eagerness to satisfy the demands of his political supporters, Perón, despite the extremely low procurement prices, further subsidized bread and meat sold to domestic consumers. Such a low-price policy is bound to stimulate consumption and hamper production—the economic rule is simple enough: the population is encouraged to buy more, the farmers are encouraged to produce less. A gap between supply and demand developed and widened continuously.

Among meat exporters Argentina for decades ranked first, but in 1950 it was surpassed by New Zealand and in 1952 by Denmark, both smaller countries. During the 1950s and 1960s Argentina held on to that position as one of the three largest meat exporters of the world, but in the 1970s its position declined drastically and by 1981 it was reduced to number ten. Ironically, Perón had believed he would be able to increase meat production by forbidding the peasants to slaughter their calves.

Argentina's meat prices strongly stimulated consumption, and in order to save some quantities for export, Perón—without raising prices —tried to check domestic consumption by instituting in 1951 and 1952 a meat-rationing system in which meat was not to be sold in stores or served in restaurants two days a week. Despite these restrictions, the Argentine average per-person consumption of beef and pork in the early 1950s was over 220 pounds (a world record), while the corresponding quantity in the United States was 165 pounds and in Great Britain about 110 pounds.

The production of meat is very resource-consuming, and, because of that, beef and pork are very expensive foodstuffs. When by its price and subsidy policies the Argentine government stimulated consumption to such an extent that the per-capita consumption of Argentina, a poor country, was substantially higher than the per-capita consumption of the United States, the most wealthy country of the world, the economic policy indicated incredible waste.

By 1946 Perón established a five-year plan in which immense resources were used to subsidize the luxury consumption of meat, resources that were most urgently needed for investment in Argentina's underdeveloped industry. According to the plan, rapid industrialization was Perón's primary goal, but given the great amounts of scarce resources allocated for pure luxury consumption, it is clear that this policy was, all along, quite inconsistent with an industrialization policy. In the Argentine case, planning evidently was not a rational exercise.

The Perón policy also affected grain production, and severe crop failures followed in 1949, 1950, and 1951. Bad weather and droughts were officially cited as the cause. The truth is that the acreage of wheat planted in these years fell so low that corresponding figures can only be found during the early years of the century. In 1951 the wheat crop was only 40 percent of the preceding year's; the linseed harvest was reduced to 10 percent. Still worse, exports of maize in 1951 fell to 3 percent and wheat to 2 percent of their prewar volume. The drastic shrinkage of exports inevitably meant a drastic shrinkage of imports, and since the country's industry is highly dependent on imported commodities, severe cuts in production could not be avoided.

Perón's Road to Crisis and Chaos

Argentina is a rich and sparsely populated country, 23 million people on 2.5 million square kilometers. That everything went so wrong in this country is one of the great mysteries of our time.

V. S. Naipaul, British author, 1973

Finally, virtually everything was in short supply—meat, bread, butter, milk, wine, cheese, salt, sugar, coffee, tea, grain, even matches. The low, controlled prices, out of touch with reality, had rendered the situation untenable. Black markets gradually took over distribution.

Argentines began to express strong dissatisfaction with the rapidly rising prices. The powerful Peronist-controlled CGT—the General Confederation of Labor—finally forced Perón to take strong measures against the businessmen and shopowners who had violated the price-control decrees. Hundreds of food shops closed, their owners arrested and sentenced to prison. This time the socialists made businessmen and shopowners the scapegoats for the government's absurd and devastating policies. And persecution of private enterprise only made the supply problem even worse.

Because the situation was steadily deteriorating, Perón moved the presidential election up from February 1952 to November 1951. His reelection secure, Perón felt strong enough to begin his new term by correcting some of the worst mistakes of his earlier economic policy. To strengthen the production incentives of the peasants, procurement prices were radically increased in the spring of 1952. And to reduce the exploding budgetary deficits, most of the food subsidies were eliminated. As could have been expected, something of a price explosion followed.

Initially, Perón tried to pay for the extensive system of public welfare by emptying the large foreign-exchange reserves that had accumulated during World War II and by borrowing heavily abroad. Nevertheless, he could not prevent stagnation and a steady deterioration into economic chaos. He tried to compensate his political supporters, the industrial workers, for galloping inflation by initiating wage increases, but the austerity policy introduced in 1952 spurred popular dissatisfaction to new heights. Demonstrations and strikes followed, bringing Perón into conflict with his own supporters. When a general railway strike paralyzed the country's transportation system, Perón threatened to punish the strikers severely if they did not return to work.

As mentioned earlier, the military were critical of Perón's socialist policies from the beginning, but he tried hard to win military support by placing heavy emphasis on defense and by granting generous privileges to the officers. But despite Perón's favors, the army was not a reliable political ally. As often happens when a political regime pursues a policy that threatens economic disaster, the military considered it their duty to interfere and install a new regime.

The Argentine army did not act, however, until 1955, when they forced Perón to resign and to leave the country. The army revolt was supported by the Catholic Church and by the liberal opposition, while the sympathies of the workers and the trade unions were still with Perón, "the nation's leading worker." Even during the years of his exile Perón continued to exert strong political power in Argentina, and in 1973 after eighteen years in exile, Perón won a landslide election victory, which enabled him to return in triumph. During his exile, however, he had aged—he was seventy-eight and seriously ill. The following year he died. After his death, his widow provisionally assumed power.

During the second Peronist period, which began in 1973, the party pursued a policy that strongly favored the workers at the expense of the peasants, and as a result the economic situation rapidly deteriorated. In 1976, with inflation galloping at the rate of 300 to 400 percent a year, with economic stagnation and chaos at Argentina's doorstep, the military took power and brought the Peronist regime to its end for the second time.

The Perón Legacy

Despite internal tensions and mistakes Peronism has survived all crises. It is still as natural for Argentine workers to vote Peronist as it is for workers in Western Europe to vote socialist or communist.

Christer Morling, Swedish journalist, 1982

Although in 1955 Perón was deposed, Peronism was in no way finished in Argentina. The Peronist party, whose power was based on the political support of the industrial workers and their unions, pursued a policy that made of its supporters a privileged calss. A privileged class is always prepared to fight tooth and nail for its privileges. And easy as it is for a regime to grant favors to a certain class, it is difficult for another regime to deprive that class of the privileges they have come to know and which they regard as part and parcel of the natural order. The workers Perón had favored were organized into strong trade unions and were prepared to attack "social disarmament" and to defend their privileges. When a new government in 1955 inherited a bankrupt society from the first Peronist regime, it is not surprising that it could not eliminate the privileges and establish a sound economy. And the difficulties were no less severe for the governments that took over in 1976, after the end of the second Peronist regime. A legal ban on the General Confederation of Labor issued in 1976 did not change matters very much.

Since 1976 the various military governments have, with limited success, pursued a liberal economic policy. In an attempt to restore a market economy, they have, among other things, sold shares in previously socialized companies on the open market. Protests against this "capitalist" policy became so strong, however, that in the spring of 1982 the government had to stop the sales. Even military juntas prepared to employ weapons and force to defend their power are as intent as populist regimes on trying to win the sympathy and support of the masses.

Since 1946, Perón's first year as president, the Argentines have had to live with galloping inflation. Between 1946 and 1982, the value of the national currency, the peso, fell to a hundred-thousandth of its former value in relation to the dollar. With average price increases of more than 100 percent a year, the rate of inflation in Argentina for the years 1981, 1982, and 1983 was the highest in the world. When the price increases reached a rate of 433% in 1983, the record set in 1976 was surpassed. Raul Alfonsín, who won the presidential elections in 1983, promised that if he were elected he would keep the rate of inflation below 100% in 1984—a difficult promise for Argentina to keep.

In 1970 the government resolved to substitute a new peso for the old inflation-stricken one. The new peso was equal to 100 old pesos. In 1983 time was ripe for a new currency reform, and this time the new peso was equal to 10,000 old pesos. Instead of paying 15,000 old pesos for a cup of coffee, you paid the seemingly more reasonable 1.50.

Disastrous declines in exports and imports had plagued Argentina since the 1950s. But severe shortages and bottlenecks finally crippled industry and it was unable to operate at more than half its capacity. During the 1980s, according to observers, unemployment increased to approximately 20 percent—official figures were lower, and the standard of living fell to a level equal to about 60 percent of its earlier level. When shrinking exports became insufficient to pay for necessary imports, the successive governments tried to maintain import volume through hefty loans from abroad. When the military Argentine governments from 1976 to 1983 increased the foreign debt from $8 billion to $40 billion, they fell victim to the narcotic of borrowing to alleviate and postpone economic and social pains.

Its population figuring at 28 million in 1983, Argentina had a foreign debt that amounted to $40 billion—a debt larger per capita than those of Brazil, Mexico, and Poland. That same year, Argentina's debt-service payments consumed 150 percent of the country's export income. What must be considered a miracle is that until 1982 Argentine governments largely were able to meet their payment obligations; the flow of new loans made it possible. As late as October 1982 the IMF granted Argentina an emergency loan of $2 billion. The loan, however, was not without its stipulations; it demanded more austere government policies. In October 1983 IMF announced that these conditions had not been fulfilled and concluded that all further lending to Argentina was to be canceled. The IMF declaration signaled private banks abroad to stop further lending. That signal was final confirmation of Argentinian bankruptcy.

But the Peronist legacy bequeathed even more. Argentina, a country very rich in natural resources, had been—until 1930—one of the world's foremost immigration states, a land that had welcomed some 6 million immigrants during the preceding fifty years. In recent years, however, domestic conditions have become so trying that many have preferred to leave the country. Today Argentina is an emigration country; in the course of a few years more than 2 million people—8 percent of the population—have simply left. As these largely are educated people, this emigration represents a serious "brain drain" for the country.

Lessons from the Peronist Experiment

> Argentina cannot become a democratic state until Peronism has disappeared. But Peronism will not disappear until Argentina has become a democratic state.
>
> *Buenos Aires Herald,* May 11, 1982

Soil and climate have given Argentina a position among the four foremost agricultural countries of the world. It has natural resources, moreover, such as iron, copper, and oil, which are important industrial assets. And 90 percent of its adult population is literate.

The Peronist experiment demonstrates the fact that no natural resources in the world are sufficient guarantee for a favorable standard of living; that an unsound economic policy will convert wealth into poverty. The Peronist experiment demonstrates further the apparently insurmountable difficulties encountered by a new regime that tries to reintroduce a market economy by reducing the public welfare system to proportions that the country can pay for with its own production and exports.

Welfare systems, following growth patterns built into their constructs, seem bound to develop elephantiasis and, therefore, bound to be crushed by their own weight. The crucial question is whether the final crash could be prevented by a reform policy that gradually dismantles the welfare colossus. In Sri Lanka, as we saw earlier, the welfare system ran its course to the bitter end. The regime responsible for the system was allowed to stay in power until the crash came. The new anti-privilege government did not have to take away privileges or reduce public welfare. Before it had taken over, the runaway system had collapsed, and so the new regime could concentrate on the popular task of restoring a state in ruins.

In contrast, the new government that took over in Argentina after the demise of the second Peronist regime in 1976 inherited a top-heavy privilege system and felt duty-bound to try to prevent a crash by implementing an austerity policy. The privileged groups, however, defended their privileges so fiercely that only limited portions of the austerity program could be effected. The new regime could stay in power only because of its strong military support. Oddly enough, the state-of-emergency laws introduced by the Peronist regime in 1974 were upheld until October 1983 by the anti-Peronist governments that succeeded it.

Since the 1976 coup, military officers have governed the country as presidents. When President Roberto Viola, the second of them, was deposed in December 1981 after only eight months in office, his adversaries cited his complete failure to solve the worst economic crisis in Argentina's 165-year history.

President Viola's successor, General and Commander-in-Chief Leopoldo Galtieri, ordered the occupation of the Falkland Islands four months later, on April 2, 1982—obviously a diversionary political maneuver, an effort to draw attention away from the economic chaos in the country. The action proved a political success initially, since the entire population—including the Peronists, otherwise bitter enemies of military regime—hailed the occupation with patriotic fervor. But war with Great Britain ensued. When Argentina's army surrendered in June after 1,366 casualties, General Galtieri had to leave the presidential palace and the political scene. He was succeeded by a retired general of the army, Reynaldo Bignone, who tried to pursue an "offensive and expansive" economic policy—the opposite of the previous unpopular austerity policy—in the hopes of avoiding confrontations with the Peronists. No concessions could appease the masses, however. On December 16, 1982, 100,000 Argentines demonstrated against the military regime on the Plaza de Mayo in Buenos Aires—the very masses who a few months earlier had hailed the same military regime for their courageous occupation of the Falkland Islands.

After the defeat in the Falklands, with all liquid reserves exhausted and with galloping inflation accompanying the worst economic crisis in Argentine history, the military regime at long last had to surrender. In December 1982 they promised the Argentine people democratic elections before the end of 1983, after which power would be transferred into the hands of a civil government. The elections were set for October 30, 1983, and would be the first general election in ten years; the new government would take over in December 1983.

In the October elections the Radical party—contrary to all forecasts —won an absolute majority with 52 percent of the votes; the Peronist party had to be satisfied with 40 percent. Ten years before, in the 1973 elections, the shares of the two parties had been 24 for the Radicals and 62 percent for the Peronists. When for the first time in their history the Peronists lost an election, the defeat could be attributed primarily to the gulf between theory and practice in Peronist policies. Their two terms of power had ended in complete economic collapse, and the honeymoon with the Argentine people was clearly over.

In order to attract middle-class votes, the Peronist party never declared itself a socialist party. Officially, it was above all a nationalist welfare-state party, but this did not prevent it from pursuing socialist policies. In this respect, it was certainly not a unique phenomenon; in many welfare states, "bourgeois" parties have pursued socialist policies.

Argentines who at earlier elections had supported the Peronists now gave their votes to the Radicals evidently because they felt that decidedly new policies were needed. And as the Radicals generally are labeled rightist and the Peronists leftist, the 1983 elections may mark a turning point in Argentine political history.

When in December 1983 the new president Raul Alfonsin and his new Radical government assumed power, they faced extremely difficult economic and social problems. In 1984 $14 billion in foreign debts will fall due for payment; this in addition to $7 billion which fell due in 1982 and 1983. Without new loans, Argentina will not be able to pay a single one of these billions, and new credits will most certainly be very limited in amount. To add to the bleak economic picture, the manufacturing industry in December 1983 was utilizing only a fraction of its potential, due to lack of fuel, raw material, and spare parts. Agriculture, due to earlier exploitation, was producing at half speed.

The Argentines have to start from scratch. They must shoulder hard work and suffer deprivations before they can build a new production machinery out of the ruins. Their only solution lies in a hard austerity policy—a bitter medicine the Argentines will find difficult to swallow. As it is, they express their protest and desperation by staging general strikes. The general strike on October 4, 1983, was the third general strike that year. Every strike, to be sure, means only less production and worse shortages. But the demonstrators seem quite unconscious of the causal relations between their own political behavior and the present crisis. The industrial workers and the urban population, the supporters of the Perón governments, have always demanded cheap food as a privilege. They are unaware that when they were granted cheap food by the populist Peronist governments, the privilege was given them at the expense of the peasants. And it was the exploitation of the peasants that destroyed the entrepreneurial environment in Argentine agriculture. This oppression of the peasant will surely have to be changed if Argentina means to address its crisis.

PART III

Crises and Entrepreneurship in the West

Many countries around the world are today experiencing socially destructive inflation, abnormally high unemployment, misuse of economic resources, and, in some cases, the suppression of human freedom, not because evil men deliberately sought to achieve these results, nor because of differences in values among their citizens, but because of erroneous judgments about the consequences of government measures: errors that at least in principle are capable of being corrected by the progress of positive economic science.

Milton Friedman, Nobel Laureate, 1976

Chapter 17

Capitalism and Economic Crisis

> We are in the deepest crisis since the 1930s, perhaps even worse, and extraordinarily severe hardships await us in the future.
>
> *Gunnar Myrdal,* Nobel Laureate, 1978

Capitalism's "Last" Crisis in the 1930s

> If History herself were a fellow-traveller, she could not have arranged a more clever timing of events than this coincidence of the gravest crisis of the Western world with the initial phase of Russia's industrial revolution.
>
> *Arthur Koestler,* 1952

An obvious characteristic of the economic crises of both the 1930s and the 1970s—still rolling on in the 1980s—is their simultaneous appearance in various countries, a simultaneity which suggests a common cause. Today it seems clear that the only possible cause is the economic policy pursued in the crisis countries.

There are fashions not only in clothes but in economic policies. Governments in different countries pursue virtually the same policies

—the same monetary policy, the same tax policy, the same public welfare policy, the same employment policy—almost irrespective of the political color of the regime.

All of us are indoctrinated with the theories of our own age, ideas and evaluations in the socioeconomic field, as in other areas. We behave, in fact, like captives of our own mental straitjackets—as if only a few among us were able to liberate ourselves and think freely.

From the very beginning, cyclical economic fluctuations were to be observed in the economies of the industrial countries—fluctuations between booms and slumps that tended to grow continuously in strength. Karl Marx studied these cycles with great interest and concluded that the capitalist system's depressions, with their "technologically" caused mass unemployment, would eventually accelerate to the point of collapse. And for a long time Marx appeared to be right. While earlier slumps—even the devastating postwar depression of the early 1920s—were soon followed by better times, recovery was delayed in the Great Depression of the 1930s. As years passed in the thirties, more and more people in many countries came to believe that mass unemployment had come to stay—that it had become a chronic social disease. In 1938, the last prewar year, unemployment still stood at 19 percent in the United States.

During the 1930s, when there was only one socialist state, and when only the capitalist world was struck by depression, socialists all over the world rehearsed funeral hymns for the expected burial of the fatally ill capitalist patient. Simultaneously, triumphant trumpet calls were heard from the East, where the first Soviet five-year plan had been launched in the autumn of 1928. In the West there were mass unemployment and economic paralysis; in the East an explosion of investment and expansion, an economic eruption that brought not only full employment but even a shortage of labor. The contrast could not have been more striking. In his autobiography Arthur Koestler depicted the situation thus:

> In Russia the First Five Year Plan was transforming, by a series of giant strokes, the most backward into the advanced country in Europe . . . The contrast between the downward trend of capitalism and the simultaneous steep rise of planned Soviet economy was so striking and obvious that it led to the equally obvious conclusion: They are the future—we, the past.[1]

Capitalism's Present Crisis

> Every ruling class develops a mythology, justifying its abuse of power and its exploitation of the subjects.
>
> *Karl Marx,* 1848

If we compare the depression of the 1930s to the depression[2] that developed fully in the 1970s and is still going on in the 1980s, the most remarkable difference is that in the current crisis both the capitalist and socialist worlds have been affected. That fact suggests the possibility of a common cause. Since either side has a strong ideological interest in presenting a different profile, the two tend to exaggerate their differences and to minimize their similarities. In reality the capitalist welfare states of the West and the socialist welfare states of the East differ less than is generally believed.

As the fundamental thesis of this book would have it, the roots of the crises must be sought in governmental policies that kill production incentives. In the socialist world this is most conspicuously demonstrated in agriculture; in the capitalist world it is most conspicuously demonstrated elsewhere.

Let us begin by stating that all entrepreneurial activity involves risks of losses and chances of winnings like a game or a lottery. If people are willing to risk losses, the chances of winning must be good enough to outweigh the risks. In a lottery it is the largest prizes that attract participants; the same is true of industrial enterprise. The largest prizes—profits—are rare, but they are indispensable as incentives. Significant for the modern Western welfare states, in which consumers and employees constitute a political majority and possess substantial political power—the state coercion apparatus—is that this majority, especially during the last ten to fifteen years, has pursued policies that militate against the minority of entrepreneurs. The substance of these policies is summarized in the following two points:

- Because of successive increases in taxes and fees, profits—primarily large profits—have been reduced continuously, and entrepreneurial incentives have been weakened.
- Entrepreneurs have been placed in straitjackets whose fabric is woven from hundreds of state regulations, jackets that have de-

prived them of that maneuvering space without which they cannot function. And the jackets have been continually "improved" with tighter and tighter controls.

Since the late 1960s, Western governments produced new regulation laws at an accelerating speed. Behind all these laws imposing increased taxes and regulations on entrepreneurs there is, to be sure, an element of envy. Successful entrepreneurs can be wealthy persons with high incomes and conspicuous consumption habits. This small minority of people becomes the characterization for the whole class of entrepreneurs; the majority with moderate incomes goes unheeded. Concerning the possible economic consequences of envy Ludwig von Mises once said:

> Many people are utterly unfit to deal with the phenomenon of entrepreneurial profit without indulging in envious resentment. In their eyes the source of profit is exploitation of the wage earners and the consumers. . . . Economics merely establishes the fact that entrepreneurial profits and losses are essential phenomena of the market economy. There cannot be a market economy without them. It is certainly possible for the police to confiscate all profits. But such a policy would by necessity convert the market economy into a senseless chaos. Man has, there is no doubt, the power to destroy many things, and he has made in the course of history ample use of this faculty. He could destroy the market economy too.[3]

Maybe an economic "law" concerning envy could be formulated: A society whose members are too envious to safeguard the rights of those who succeed will lack the resources to support those who fail.

Irrespective of the driving forces behind the policies pursued, the majorities in power seem to be quite unconscious that their policies may imply oppression for the entrepreneurial minority group. The idea has simply never occurred to them. Decisions have been made by government majorities by a process of "democratic order." It is not surprising, then, that powers-that-be in recent times have felt no responsibility for the economic crisis their incentive-killing policies have produced. Their ingenuity in producing pseudoexplanations and scapegoats is impressive. This purblindness is well in accordance with established psychological patterns. All oppressors and exploiters in history seem to have been people with clear consciences, people sleeping well at night, people firmly convinced of the justice and beneficial effects of their policies. More surprising is the fact that the victims are equally unconscious of the real implications of the policies pursued; they do not feel oppressed and exploited. They experience their society with its institutions as belonging to the "natural order," and like all citizens they are indoctrinated to accept its laws and policies. According to reports from feudal societies, serfs and slaves did not experience themselves as oppressed and exploited either. As a rule they looked upon serfdom and slavery as natural social systems. Israel Kirzner has observed this typical unconsciousness in many contexts, and in his book *Perception, Opportunity, and Profit* he described it as follows:

A broader understanding of the meaning of freedom, and of its loss, makes it entirely plausible that abrogations of freedom may indeed affect individuals without being aware or for that matter without the awareness of anyone else, observing social scientists included, that their welfare has been damaged by this abrogation. It is no longer a necessary condition for the existence of loss of freedom that the loss be a felt one.[4]

From this unconsciousness it follows that the majorities executing or supporting parasitic policies find it difficult to ascertain the real causes of the problems when backlash and "retribution" finally come. This is exemplified by the Polish situation in which the urban population, including the industrial workers, continuously demand cheap food, and so support the government's parasitic policies against the peasants. When severe food shortages were finally evident, the blinders were donned, and Poles found themselves squarely rejecting responsibility for the shortages and blaming the victims—the peasants—instead.

Similarly, the parasitic policies mounted against the entrepreneur in the West have enjoyed continuous support from the wage-earners and their trade unions—that majority of the population now suffering the inevitable consequences of shrinking production, declining standards of living, and growing unemployment. The same psychological mechanisms, the same blinders, are keeping this segment from seeing and admitting their own responsibility. Instead, they accuse the victims, the entrepreneurs, of sluggishness and of lacking the will to invest. When the economic situation became so critical as to force entrepreneurs to discharge employees or even to close their firms, they were labeled bad managers lacking in social responsibility.

Socialists in the West, the most active supporters of parasitic policies, interpret the present crisis as decisive proof that private enterprise is incapable of managing production and employment, that capitalism is bankrupt, that it is a system now passing into its final crisis, ripe for the rubbish heap of history.

Instead of re-creating a favorable entrepreneurial environment by restoring economic freedom, the majorities in power have tried to stimulate industry by allocating gigantic amounts of tax money to ailing enterprises. But trying to accelerate a sluggish industry by applying state subsidies is a bit like towing a car and expecting the motion alone to be enough: Until the engine has been repaired, the car cannot be expected to run.

Redistribution of Existing Jobs

Unemployment occupies more and more people.

Giscard d'Estaing, 1979

It must be acknowledged that the Western groups in power have done their utmost to increase the supply of jobs in order to eliminate unemployment. But despite enormous state investments and subsidies to ailing enterprises—with enormous budgetary deficits as a consequence—unemployment has demonstrated a total immunity to the cures. Quite unaffected, the malady has only spread and reached such proportions that in most Western countries today it is appropriate to speak of mass unemployment.

Of course the economic doctors defend their failure by dredging up the classic defense used by failing medical doctors: Had the cures not been applied, the malady would have been even worse. Nonetheless, politicians searched desperately for scapegoats on whom to load the responsibility; at long last they found one and baptized it "long-term structural changes." At closer inspection it was recognized as the "technological unemployment" invented by Marx and last in service during the 1930s: When more and more sophisticated machines are substituted for workers, more and more unemployment is created. During a period of mass unemployment, it seems that most people find this explanation credible.

During the Second World War and the following decades of full employment, there was no need for such explanations, and so Marx's "technological unemployment" like an outdated garment was stuffed back into the wardrobe. Despite the increasing production of sophisticated machines capable of replacing more and more workers, this imposing technological development did not prevent full employment during the three decades from 1940 to 1970. And during this long period, full employment was a product of the market forces; government interferences were few.

In the early 1970s the ghost of technological unemployment still languished in the wardrobe, but by the late 1970s and especially during the mass unemployment years of the 1980s, the old notion was resurrected and generally accepted as a probable explanation of unemployment. The scapegoat had served well during many an unemployment period, the first one during the early decades of the industrial revolution in Great Britain. The new mechanical spinning machine and looms were technological miracles. One single worker on a spinning machine could produce as much yarn as two hundred homeworkers using manual spinning wheels. Unemployed homeworkers were so frightened and desperate that they attacked hundreds of factories and destroyed the machines.

In the long perspective, their fear and rage was unjustified. Employment in the British cotton industry actually increased from 40,000 in the 1750s to 800,000 in the 1830s. And this increase occurred despite the sophisticated machines, despite their increasing numbers, and despite the fact that they had become more and more efficient "and labor-saving."

Since the eighteenth century the "technological unemployment" excuse has reared its head many times, and its supporters every time have emphasized that the machines were much more advanced and efficient "this time" than they had been in previous times. In the 1980s the Cassandras point to the new electronics and robots which they claim will replace multitudes of workers and create mass unemployment that will only grow in the future.

Skeptics could point to Japan, a country which has invested more lavishly in electronics, dators, and robots than any other country and which nevertheless has suffered mild unemployment. Or they could cite the "gang of four," the miracle countries in the Far East—Singapore, Hong Kong, Taiwan, and South Korea—all of which invested in free markets and favorable entrepreneurial environments.

The technological development that has proceeded since the eighteenth century is in recent days presented as a *fundamental structural change*, bound to substitute machines for workers, bound to deprive more citizens of their jobs, bound to produce more unemployment. And, finally, bound to produce a new class society made up of a shrinking privileged upper class with jobs and a burgeoning lower class, a proletariat without jobs.

It is only natural for people who believe in this horrible vision to feel indignant, and to demand that the upper class in the name of justice and equality share their abundance with the unemployed. Those who work eight hours a day should be satisfied with, say, six hours. The two sacrificed hours could be distributed among those without jobs. The Mitterrand government in France has implemented just such a policy. It has reduced the work week from 40 to 39 hours—a further reduction from 39 to 35 is planned and promised—it has increased vacation holidays from four weeks to five, and has lowered the retirement age from 65 to 60. Despite such redistribution reforms, unemployment has only steadily grown since Mitterrand took over.

There is a basic fallacy in this sort of thinking. The mistake is in the idea that there is a stock of jobs, a constant natural resource, and that these can be distributed at will by whatever group is in power. Economists carefully distinguish between *stock* and *flow*. The jobs available in a country are not a stock but a flow, continuously created by entrepreneurs and producers, the volume of which at any time is dependent on the prevailing ecological situation, the supply of incentives.

Since the industrial revolution in the eighteenth century, the work week in industrially developing countries has been gradually shortened from six days to five and the work day from twelve to seven or eight hours. With increasing living standards, people are generally willing to substitute leisure hours for working hours by partially sacrificing wage increases. The dream of less toil and shorter working hours is age-old. In 1516 Thomas More in his book *Utopia* pleaded for six-hour working days and equality between the sexes in the labor market.

In a country such as the United States, the shorter work week has developed almost entirely as a result of free bargaining between employers and employees. In a country like Sweden, the development has been controlled by the government. Technological development and the implementation of efficient, "labor-saving" machines has made it possible for the same work force to gradually increase the production of goods, and so gradually increase the standard of living. Productivity gains were such that more leisure hours could be afforded the workers. It should be emphasized, however, that agreements between employers and employees concerning shorter work weeks seldom were perceived as measures to create more jobs. The shorter work week was intended only to create a higher standard of living. A shorter work week as a road to more jobs—via division and redistribution of existing jobs—was typical only of periods with exceptionally high unemployment such as the 1930s and the 1980s. Those who seek to solve fundamental unemployment problems by redistribution of existing jobs will inevitably find that every year there will be not only less and less to redistribute but also less and less to consume.

According to Marx and his modern followers, technological development that employs sophisticated and efficient machines is bound to produce continuously growing unemployment. Steadily increasing unemployment plus steadily aggravating economic crises were, according to Marx, bound to produce a final crisis that would bring about the total collapse of the capitalist system. Out of the ashes of this system a socialist society would rise like a Phoenix toward the sky.

The Keynesian employment theories launched in the 1930s turned out to exhibit great similarities to the Marxian theories. Neither Marx nor Keynes believed that the capitalist system with its free enterprise and free markets could produce full employment. But while Marx believed in—and hoped for—a final catastrophe for the system, Keynes hoped it could be saved. The only savior he could imagine was the government, which by means of borrowing—deficit financing—would be able to overcome the natural underemployment by means of extensive public works.

For believing socialists, the Marxian apocalyptic vision was an optimistic theory quite in accordance with their dreams and hopes. For believers in capitalism, however, the theory was a pessimistic one. For them the theory of entrepreneurship offered an optimistic alternative, a theory refuting the possibility of technological unemployment. The supply of savings, investment, and capital is, according to this theory, not the deciding factor in production and employment. The theory asks that one further step in the causal chain be taken: that the supply of production incentives, the entrepreneurial environment, is the deciding factor. It is this that will affect the rate of savings and investment and, thereby, the level of employment.

Experiences from history—especially from "miracle" periods described in previous sections of this book—demonstrate that favorable entrepreneurial environments boasting economic freedom and adequate production incentives have always been able to produce full employment.

If you accept the conclusion that the roots of the present mass unemployment are to be found in the incentive-killing policies pursued during the last ten to fifteen years by the governments in the Western welfare states, you also have to accept the conclusion that full employment can be restored as soon as the incentive-killing policies are reversed into incentive-producing policies—that is, as soon as the present unfavorable entrepreneurial environment is restored to the state that reigned in the 1960s.

Entrepreneurs and Employees

> The entrepreneurial function, the striving of entrepreneurs after profits, is the driving power in the market economy. Profit and loss are the devices by means of which the consumers exercise their supremacy on the market.
>
> *Ludwig von Mises,* 1949

One of the fundamental characteristics of a free market is the balance of power between the two parties of the market, the sellers and the buyers. Freedom of contracts and free prices ensure that one party will not force conditions on the other. Every transaction and all cooperation must be voluntary.

In free markets, free prices will adapt to any changes in the supply and demand so that a near market equilibrium is maintained. Because price adaptations are not abrupt but take place after time lags, even in free markets one can observe minor deviations from equilibrium: At times the supply can be characterized as "abundant," at others as more "scarce." But in free markets, such deviations are always limited.

As soon as governments interfere in the market and apply their coercive apparatus to fix prices or to decide special conditions for production, consumption, or distribution, the market equilibrium will be disturbed. The only exception is when government fixes prices or decides conditions that would have spontaneously occurred in the market. If prices are fixed *below* the free market level, production incentives will be weaker and consumption incentives stronger. A shortage is bound to follow, as it does and has done with food in socialist countries. If prices are fixed *above* the free market level, production incentives will be stronger and consumption incentives weaker. A surplus becomes inevitable, as is typical with food in capitalist countries.

As soon as the balance between supply and demand is disturbed, the balance of power between sellers and buyers is disturbed, too. In a shortage, the buyers find themselves in a weak bargaining position, while in a surplus situation their bargaining position is strengthened. A shortage market is a sellers' market, a surplus market is a buyers' market.

A labor market marred by unemployment is a market with a surplus of labor, a market where sellers of labor, the wage-earners, are in a weak bargaining position against the buyers, the employers. The *beati possidentes* who have jobs are all too conscious of the difficulties for the unemployed, and so they cling to their jobs accepting conditions and treatments they would never accept in a labor market with full employment. Similarly, the unemployed in a labor market that offers few jobs have to accept wages and conditions they never would accept in a balanced labor market. Of course, the employers, able to choose among long lines of applicants, have a strong position. Employers are buyers of labor, and a labor market beset with unemployment is a buyers' market.

Groups in power who, through incentive-killing policies, have brought about unemployment feel pressured by their enraged constituencies to try to restore the balance of power between sellers and buyers in the labor market. The political pressure on governments can be strong and compelling. Holding governmental reins, such groups in power inevitably resort to the coercion apparatus, hoping to solve the problem through new laws.

In Sweden, the Social Democratic government in 1974 enacted job security laws, according to which personnel could be dismissed only if the firm was bankrupt or forced to reduce personnel in order to survive. Through these laws, the government tried to increase the security for that upper class in the labor market that already held jobs. But these laws made the situation worse for the lower class, the proletariat of the unemployed, because employers were reluctant to hire new staff. If a new employee showed himself unfit for the job, the employer would have insufficient reason to dismiss him. It was better not to hire at all.

The purpose of the new laws was to ensure greater security for the employees, an advantage won at the expense of the employers. More security for the employees meant less security for the employers. And a law denying security to the employers meant a law that would stifle production incentives, produce still more unemployment, and, so, continue to undermine the wage-earners. The governmental remedies meant to cure were only aggravating the patient's misery.

Let us finally consider the situation of the employees in a labor market with full employment, a market with a shortage of labor, a sellers' market. Such a market is something of a dream for job-seekers: The dilemma for the unemployed is not finding a job but choosing among the offers. In such a market, both employees with jobs and job-seekers are well aware of their strong bargaining position—they are not inferior to management, they are vital. In such a market, the employer must listen to complaints and suggestions from his employees and must try to satisfy them. An employer who refuses or fails to do so very soon has neither employees nor enterprise. In a market with high unemployment, an employer who violates written job security laws risks punishment by fine or even jail; in a market with full employment, an employer who violates unwritten market laws by refusing to satisfy reasonable employee demands risks losing his business entirely.

Full employment is possible only in countries that grant the entrepreneurs favorable environments. Such a policy favors not only the employers but the employees; both are made to feel secure and satisfied.

No law can promote job security comparable to that in countries that enjoy full employment. Employees in free labor markets with healthy employment rates know more freedom, equality, and human dignity than in any other system.

Farmers in the West

> The agriculture of the Western world is one of the economic miracles of our time. With only a small fraction of the labor force it produces more than enough for the highest consumption level of the world.
>
> *Sumner H. Schlichter,* 1957

Farmers are producers of special significance. People can do without industrial products if they have to, but food—and therefore farmers—

are indispensable. The farmer is an entrepreneur, however, and depends on favorable economic environments as much as any other entrepreneur. Any society that does not offer its farmers adequate production incentives will inevitably encounter serious trouble.

The agrarian revolution, like the industrial revolution, was sparked by favorable entrepreneurial environments. In many countries, the peasants were given the opportunity to break out of old village collectives to become free farmers, with full ownership of their land. When the farmers became free, their creative powers were released—they began to experiment with new methods of cultivation and with selective breeding of plants and animals. When these pioneers were successful, the sluggish masses followed.

A miraculous development in productivity began, reflected in the continuously shrinking fraction of the labor force employed in agriculture. While in poor industrially undeveloped countries about 90 percent of the work force must concentrate in agriculture in order to cover the food needs of the population, today, in highly developed countries like the United States and Sweden, only about 5 percent of the work force is in agriculture. And these statistics are even more dramatic when we consider that more than half of this 5 percent are part-time farmers regularly employed outside agriculture, so the net figure is actually 3 to 4 percent. However, to arrive at a realistic perception of the percentage of our labor force working in food production, we should add the workers in industries that produce such items as machines, fertilizers, and buildings for farmers. The comprehensive figure for the agricultural work force in the United States or Sweden, embracing both agriculture and infrastructures, would amount to 5 percent of the population.

That this modest percentage has been able to produce enough foodstuffs for domestic needs as well as substantial quantities for export represents extraordinary production efficiency. Many wonder how such performance is possible in these two countries where, since the 1930s, agriculture has been subjected to extensive governmental regulations. In socialist countries, after all, governmental regulations have had fatal consequences for production efficiency in agriculture. And, it must be added, many capitalist countries—such as Canada—have highly efficient farmers who produce substantial surpluses for export although their soil and climate are far from optimal. How can such performance be allied to the theory of entrepreneurship, and contrasted to the socialist failure presented in this book?

Entrepreneurs in Western countries function like a motor behind production, growth, and employment. For the motor to run, a favorable environment of incentive and reward is essential. The question is: Have American and Swedish farmers been offered such an environment? Although prices for agricultural products in the United States and Sweden as well as in the socialist countries have been set by the governments, the implications have been fundamentally different. In socialist countries, governments, by setting prices *below* the market level, have used price control as an instrument of exploitation against the peasants—an instrument complete with compulsory deliveries to state purchasing agencies. In the Western countries, governments, by setting prices *above* the market level, have used price control as an instrument to favor and protect their farmers—an instrument complete with protective tariff walls to prevent competition with food imports. Within a framework of governmentally controlled but favorable prices and governmental protection against competition from abroad, the farmers have, in fact, been able to function as free entrepreneurs with incentives so strong that they both work hard and develop their creative potential.

The production performance in Western agriculture is nothing more and nothing less than a result of incentives. This in no way means that Western farmers see themselves as a privileged group. On the contrary, they often express great bitterness at the prices that are set and the conditions that are granted. Working in a regulated industry, they are obliged to eat out of the government's hands and of course they want to get more than they actually get. It must be added that the farmer in Western democracies enjoys the freedom to organize strong pressure groups and participate in political parliamentarian activities; naturally, they have exploited these opportunities fully.

A final question: Why do groups in power in socialist countries regularly exploit their peasants—and wreak havoc with production—while groups in power in capitalist countries regularly grant their farmers favorable environments, to great advantage? A complete answer is not without its difficulties. But it is clear that socialism (with centrally controlled production) is built on parasitism, capitalism (with free markets) on symbiosis. In socialist countries, groups in power try to grant privileges to their ingroups at the expense of exploited outgroups; in capitalist countries, the balance of power between parties is ensured by free markets and exploitation is impossible.

Of course, groups in power in capitalist countries can use the coercive political apparatus to exploit outgroups—for instance, industrial entrepreneurs—by imposing taxes and state regulations on them. Such exploitation, in fact, has been the tendency in recent years, and production, wealth, and employment have all suffered. But so far, the groups in power have, on the whole, been able to resist the temptation to exploit the farmer, the agricultural entrepreneur. Nevertheless, for majorities in power who are eager to provide their voters with cheap food—as well as other privileges—the temptations to exploit a shrinking group representing few votes must be strong. So far, the enticements have been resisted. But for how long?

Capitalism and the Future

Government policies concerning industry will mainly become a question of producing a political, social, and economic environment favorable for efficiency, renovation, initiative, and creativity.

Assar Lindbeck, Swedish economist, 1983

As has been emphasized earlier, a group that succeeds in conquering political power is inclined to use that power to grant privileges to its own supporters at the expense of others. History confirms such political behavior to be general. In dictatorships—whether feudal, fascist, or socialist—power is regularly used not only to oppress but to terrorize and persecute opponents, dissidents, and other outgroups. History further indicates that oppressed and persecuted groups that succeed in gaining political power can themselves become the oppressors and persecutors.

The Christian minority, oppressed and persecuted during the early centuries of the so-called Christian era, eventually grew into a majority in power, a majority that cruelly persecuted religious dissidents—heretics. And after seizing power in 1917, the oppressed and persecuted socialists of Czarist Russia were transformed overnight into the brutal oppressors of the Soviet Union.

Apart from a greater respect for human life in democratic states, the fundamental political behavior patterns are the same: Groups that assume power will use their power to grant privileges to those whom they favor and who favor them. And in all kinds of states, those in power pursue their policies in the best possible conscience, firmly convinced that their policies are just and useful.

The political behavior patterns here depicted are fundamental to an understanding of the present economic crisis in the West. Those political majorities who, since the late 1960s, have pursued policies that have eroded the entrepreneurial environment, policies that in the 1970s ripened into a severe economic crisis, were to the last quite unconscious of the implications of their policies. If a person because of his ways— for instance, his abuse of drugs—becomes ill, he cannot be cured until he realizes the causal relationship between his ways and his illness. The problem of the present crisis is that to date neither the politicians who are responsible for the crisis nor the victims of their policies, the entrepreneurs, have been conscious of the causes.

Recently, however, a small but steadily growing minority has begun to understand the connection between the policies pursued and the crisis at hand. Not only are neoliberal and neoconservative ideas spreading, but so are ideas from the new philosophy of entrepreneurship. Evidently, the time is ripe. Even in France, with its current socialist-communist government, Laurent Fabius, who is pragmatic and pro-entrepreneurial, was instated as Minister of Industry in 1983, replacing Jean-Pierre Chevènement, who is leftist and anti-entrepreneurial; the change has had extensive effects on industrial policies.

In Sweden, Thage Peterson, a social democrat and minister of industry, in 1983 declared:

> In recent years, an appreciation for good entrepreneurial climates and decent dividends to those who invest time and energies in firms of their own, has developed within the labor movement. The Swedish labor movement is not only pro-industry but pro the entrepreneur, too.[5]

Although most entrepreneurs would object that they have experienced little practical proof of the new understanding, such a declaration is remarkable and symptomatic of the effects of the new ideas. Only a few years ago to claim to be pro-industry and pro-entrepreneur at the same time would have been unimaginable. But during the trying crisis years, people have come to comprehend the value of entrepreneurs and their effects on production, living standards, and employment. At long last people have begun to learn that entrepreneurs are a unique resource we urgently need.

NOTES

Book Epigraph
Friedrich A. Hayek, *Studies in Philosophy, Economics, and Politics* (Chicago: University of Chicago Press, 1966), 194.

Part I
Part I Epigraph
Israel M. Kirzner, "The Primacy of Entrepreneurial Discovery" in *The Prime Mover of Progress: The Entrepreneur in Capitalism and Socialism* (London: The Institute of Economic Affairs, 1980), 7, 26.

1. Eli F. Heckscher in *Dagens Nyheter*, December 24, 1951.

2. Ibid. More about the industrial revolution and its roots in John Chamberlain, *The Roots of Capitalism* (New York: D. Van Nostrand, 1959) and in Douglass North & Robert Thomas, *The Rise of the Western World: A New Economic History* (Cambridge: Cambridge University Press, 1973). North and Thomas emphasize the fundamental importance of private ownership behind all economic development, even for development that preceded the industrial revolution.

3. Paul Johnson, "Has Capitalism a Future?" *The Freeman*, January 1979.

4. Bengt Holgersson, "Cultivated Land in Sweden and Its Growth 1840–1939" in *Economy and History*, Vol. XVII (Lund: The Institute of Economic History at the University of Lund, Sweden, 1974), 20–51.

5. Edwin O. Reischauer, *Japan Past and Present*, 3rd revised edition (Tokyo: Charles E. Tuttle, 1969), 233.

6. Chiaki Nishiyama and G. C. Allen, *The Price of Prosperity: Lessons from Japan* (London: The Institute of Economic Affairs, 1974), 36.

7. Masaki Imai, *Never Take Yes for an Answer* (Tokyo: The Simul Press, 1975), 78.

8. Chie Nikane, *Japanese Society* (Berkeley and Los Angeles: University of California Press, 1970), 69, 72, 76.

9. Sven Rydenfelt, *Japan: Vad kan vi lära oss av arbetsgladjens och produktionsundrens land?* [Japan: What Can We Learn from the Land of Work Satisfaction and Production Miracles?] (Stockholm: Sveriges Marknadsförbund, 1978), 48, 49.

10. Michael Lipton, *Why Poor People Stay Poor* (London: Temple Smith, 1977).

11. Theodore Schultz, *Economic Growth and Agriculture* (New York: McGraw Hill, 1968).

12. Ronald C. Nairn, *Wealth of Nations in Crisis* (Houston: Bayland Publishing Co., 1979). Nairn demonstrates the importance of "political, economic, and social inhibitors"—that is, the importance of the entrepreneurial environment of the peasants.

13. *Scientific American*, Vol. 235 (September 1976).

14. For the arguments here presented I am indebted especially to P. T. Bauer, *Equality, The Third World, and Economic Delusion* (London: Weidenfeldt & Nicolson, 1981).

15. This prospect has been vividly depicted in Anthony Sampson, *The Money Lenders: Bankers in a Dangerous World* (London: Hodder & Stoughton, 1982).

16. Joseph A. Schumpeter, *The Theory of Economic Development* (Cambridge, Mass.: Harvard University Press, 1951), 143.

17. Joseph A. Schumpeter, *History of Economic Analysis* (New York: Oxford University Press, 1954), 556.

18. Richard G. Lipsey and Peter O. Steiner, *Economics*, 6th edition (New York: Harper & Row, 1981), 175.

19. F. A. Hayek, *Full Employment at Any Price?* (London: The Institute of Economic Affairs, 1975), 42.

20. Ludwig von Mises, *Human Action: A Treatise on Economics*, 2nd printing (New Haven: Yale University Press, 1949), 290f.

Part II

1. More about Marx's view of peasants and agriculture can be found in: David Mitrany, *Marx Against the Peasant: A Study in Social Dogmatism* (Chapel Hill: University of North Carolina Press, 1951); W. W. Rostov, "Marx Was a City Boy," *Harper's Magazine*, February 1955; and Lester R. Brown, "Karl Marx Was a City Boy," *Science*, September 12, 1980.

2. In *L'Erreur de l'Occident* (Paris: Grasset, 1980), Alexander Solzhenitsyn asserts that in Czarist Russia there "were never any slave camps—the idea as such was entirely unknown. There were only a few State prisons and that was why political prisoners—except terrorists—including the Bolsheviks, were sent into comfortable exile where they were well supported at the expense of the State, where they were not forced to work and where all who so desired could unhindered escape abroad."

3. See Roy A. Medvedev, *The October Revolution* (New York, Columbia University Press, 1979).

4. Lester R. Brown, *U.S. and Soviet Agriculture: The Shifting Balance of Power* (Worldwatch Paper 51, October 1982), 12.

5. United Nations Food and Agriculture Organization (FAO): *Production Yearbook.*

6. Brown, 11.

7. Ibid, 29. See also Karl-Eugen Wadekin, "Soviet Agriculture's Dependence on the West," *Foreign Affairs,* Spring 1982.

8. Information about Soviet private agriculture can be found in Karl-Eugen Wadekin, *The Private Sector in Soviet Agriculture* (University of California Press, 1973), and in *Neue Zurcher Zeitung,* 292/1979 and 23, 35, 59 and 82/1980.

9. *Foder och Spannmal* [Fodder and Grain], January 1975.

10. Adam Smith, *An Inquiry into the Nature and Causes of the Wealth of Nations,* ed. E. Cannan (London: Methuen & Co., 1904), vol. 1, p. 364, and vol. 2, p. 181.

11. *Trybuna Ludu,* February 20, 1981.

12. FAO: *Production Yearbook.*

13. *Svenska Dagbladet,* March 23, 1982.

14. Ibid., July 2, 1982.

15. Andres Küng, *Sådan är socialismen* [Such Is Socialism] (Stockholm: Timbro, 1982), 237.

16. *Monthly Review,* October 1968.

17. See Kirzner, 22: "We do not deny the possibility of arranging incentives to socialist managers to produce more, or to produce with a smaller labor force, or lower energy consumption. Nor do we deny the possibility of offering incentives that will reward innovation." See also Evsey D. Domar, "On the Optimal Compensation of a Socialist Manager," *Quarterly Journal of Economics,* vol. 88, February 1974, 1–18. And Mo-Yin S. Tam, "Reward Structures in a Planned Economy: The Problem of Incentives and Efficient Allocation of Resources," Ibid., vol. 96, February 1981, 111–128.

18. *Wall Street Journal,* August 2, 1983.

19. Ibid., February 14, 1971.

20. *The Economist,* April 2, 1983, 80.

21. United Nations High Commissioner for Refugees (UNHCR) reports.

22. *Le Monde,* October 17, 1978.

23. The Fifth Party Congress, March 1982.

24. Verena Stern, "Ein Wahlkamph um die Marktwirtschaft," *Die Welt,* October 16, 1982.

25. Nairn, 177.

26. Kenneth W. Banta, *Time,* February 21, 1983.

27. Mises, 758.

28. Kwame Nkrumah in his speech on Independence Day, March 6, 1957.

29. *Aftenposten,* December 9, 1981.

30. Anders Johansson, *Dagens Nyheter,* February 27, 1982.

31. Swein Wiel Jörgensen, *Ökonomisk Rapport,* October 1982.

32. *Dagens Nyheter,* October 9, 1979.

33. FAO: *Production Yearbook.*

Part III
Part III Epigraph
Milton Friedman, "Inflation and Unemployment," Nobel lecture, Stockholm, December 8, 1976. See *Journal of Political Economy,* Vol. 85 (June 1977), 451–472.

1. Arthur Koestler, *Arrow in the Blue: An Autobiography* (New York: The MacMillan Co., 1952), 277f.

2. Boileau once preferred to call a cat a cat and a scoundrel a scoundrel. In this book I prefer to call a depression a depression instead of using the euphemistic word recession. I am happy to be able to refer to George Stigler —Nobel Laureate in 1982—who in a Swedish economic journal (*Veckans affärer,* December 9, 1982) preferred to call the American economic situation in 1982 a depression, thereby rejecting the idea that this word should be reserved exclusively for the dismal years of the 1930s.

3. Mises, 295–296.

4. Israel M. Kirzner, *Perception, Opportunity, and Profit* (Chicago: University of Chicago Press, 1980), 235.

5. *Svenska Dagbladet,* August 11, 1983.

INDEX